T★∗AMERICAN∗★★ TROUBLEMAKERS

Samuel Adams: Grandfather of His Country

★★AMERICAN★★ TROUBLEMAKERS

AMERICAN TROUBLEMAKERS

SAMUEL ADAMS:
Grandfather of His Country

Karin Clafford Farley

With an Introduction by James P. Shenton

RSVP
RAINTREE STECK-VAUGHN
PUBLISHERS
The Steck-Vaughn Company

Austin, Texas

For my son, Glenn K. Farley

CONSULTANTS

Richard M. Haynes
Director, Office of Field Experiences
    and Certification
College of Education and Psychology
Western Carolina University
Cullowhee, North Carolina

Michael Kort
Professor of Social Science
Boston University
Boston, Massachusetts

MANAGING EDITOR
Richard G. Gallin

PROJECT MANAGER
Julie Klaus

PHOTO EDITOR
Margie Foster

A Gallin House Press Book

Library of Congress Cataloging-in-Publication Data
Farley, Karin Clafford
    Samuel Adams: grandfather of his country/ Karin Clafford Farley; with an introduction by James P. Shenton.
        p.   cm. — (American troublemakers)
    "A Gallin House Press Book."
    Includes bibliographical references and index.
    ISBN 0-8114-2379-4
    1. Adams, Samuel, 1722-1803 — Juvenile literature.   2. Politicians — United States — Biography — Juvenile literature.   3. United States — Declaration of Independence — Signers — Biography—Juvenile literature.
I.Title.   II. Series.
E302.6.A2F37   1995
973.3'092—dc20
[B]   94-12646
                                                                                            CIP
                                                                                            AC

Printed and bound in the United States.
1 2 3 4 5 6 7 8 9 0 LB 98 97 96 95 94

CONTENTS

Maps

Samuel Adams

by James P. Shenton

Biography is the history of the individual lives of men and women. In all lives, there is a sequence that begins with birth, evolves into the development of character in childhood and adolescence, is followed by the emergence of maturity in adulthood, and finally concludes with death. All lives follow this pattern, although with each emerge the differences that make each life unique. These distinctive characteristics are usually determined by the particular area in which a person has been most active. An artist draws his or her specific identity from the area of the arts in which he or she has been most active. So the writer becomes an author; the musician, a performer or composer; the politician, a senator, governor, president, or statesperson. The intellectual discipline to which one is attached identifies the scientist, historian, economist, literary critic, or political scientist, among many. Some aspects of human behavior are identified as heroic, cowardly, corrupt, or just ordinary. The task of the biographer is to explain why a particular life is worth remembering. And if the effort is successful, the reader draws from it insights into a vast range of behavior patterns. In a sense, biography provides lessons from life.

Some lives become important because of the position a person holds. Typical would be that of a U.S. President in which a biographer compares the various incumbents to determine their comparative importance. Without question, Abraham Lincoln was a profoundly significant President, much more so than Warren G. Harding whose administration was swamped by corruption. Others achieve importance because of their role in a particular area. So Emily Dickinson and Carl Sandburg are recognized as important poets and Albert Einstein as a great scientist.

Implicit in the choice of biographical subjects is the idea that each somehow affected history. Their lives explain something about the world in which they lived, even as they affect our lives and that of generations to come. But there is another consideration: Some lives are more interesting than those of others. Within each life is a great story that illuminates human behavior.

7

Then there are those people who are troublemakers, people whom we cannot ignore. They are the people who both upset and fascinate us. Their singular quality is that they are uniquely different. Troublemakers are irritating, perhaps frightening, frustrating, and disturbing, but never dull. They march to their own drummer, and they are original.

Samuel Adams was a rare politician who managed to work both within and outside the British colonial government in North America to subvert it. An unsuccessful businessman, he turned his attention to local Boston politics. Adams revealed a unique talent for mobilizing popular opinion against what he called the privileged orders. Colonists viewed with astonishment his scathing attacks on British laws such as the Stamp Act. His message was directed to the ordinary citizens who were thrilled by the blunt simplicity of his language.

Samuel Adams's political views catapulted him to election to the Massachusetts General Court. He was also active at the Boston town meetings. From those positions, he used his organizational skills to create a majority that supported his policies. Once in possession of power, he acted ruthlessly to strengthen a faction bent on revolution. In Boston, when he thought it necessary, he brought the mob into the streets. Skillfully, Adams escalated the confrontations with the British. Each of Great Britain's regulatory and tax measures was denounced as part of a plot to destroy colonial self-government. He preached the need for the colonies to unite to obstruct British tyranny. Samuel Adams's opposition to the garrison of British soldiers in Boston climaxed in a bloody clash, which he dubbed the Boston Massacre.

Adams's particular genius was in formulating vivid criticisms of British actions. He understood that a successful revolution required an unrelenting assault on existing authority. Moderation and compromise were alien to his thinking. Whenever opposition to the British declined, his full energy focused on reviving colonial discontent and finally demanding American independence. In the decade before the outbreak of the American Revolution, his agitation proclaimed the emergence of America as a distinct nation. In the years after independence was won, Samuel Adams was acclaimed as its grandfather.

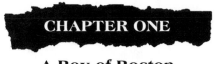

CHAPTER ONE

A Boy of Boston

W̄hen Mary Adams gave birth to her fourth child on September 16, 1722, in Boston, she insisted the infant be baptized that very afternoon. Of her other three babies, only Mary, the secondborn, now age five, was still alive. Mary Adams feared this baby might die, too. Although it was a Sunday, the baby's father carried his new son to the church and named him Samuel Adams after himself.

Thereafter, little Samuel, his sister Mary, and a brother Joseph, the Adamses' seventh child, went to church twice every Sunday. Their ears were filled with the words of fiery sermons that lasted three to five hours. Puritan clergymen were the most respected people in the colony of Massachusetts, and they had great influence. Mary Adams probably poked her oldest son to keep him awake and paying attention. It was her dearest wish to see her Samuel standing in a pulpit one day.

The elder Samuel Adams himself was a deacon of Old South Church. His considerable fortune came from the rum and ale brewing business. He was highly respected by the people of Boston not only for his wealth but for his piousness and good deeds. This respect gave him considerable influence in town matters. The spacious Adams house on Purchase Street facing Boston Harbor was a gathering place for politicians. Even as a young boy, Samuel was allowed to listen and talk to his father's political friends. Over his lifetime, Deacon Adams served as a constable, a tax assessor, and a selectman (one of the town officials). Eventually, he was elected by the town meeting of Boston to be 1 of the 112 men in the House of Representatives, the lower house of the two-house legislature known as the Massachusetts General Court. There he helped make laws for the colony.

Deacon Adams's unofficial work in government was perhaps more important. He founded the Caucus Club. Its original name

Boston's Old South Church, also known as the Old South Meeting House. Samuel Adams's father served as a deacon there.

of Caulkers Club came from the shipyard workers who were its first members. (Some of the workers actually did caulk, that is, fill in, the cracks between the wooden planks of ships in order to waterproof them. Others were carpenters or ironworkers or did other jobs in the building of vessels.) Small shopkeepers, craftsmen, and artisans later joined. While it was not a secret society, it went about its business quietly, behind the scenes. Over the years, Boston's Caucus Club came to control the politics of the town. Only citizens who owned property could vote in town elections, but Caucus Club leaders like Deacon Adams decided issues in advance of town meetings and selected the men who would run for public office. In that way, the Caucus Club gave poor working people a voice in their government.

Deacon Adams and the Caucus Club kept a sharp eye on the king and the British government. They had to so none of their special rights as colonists would be taken away. Much of the talk around the Adams house was how to protect those rights. If necessary, the Caucus Club could stir up the colonists to make trouble. The monarchs of Great Britain would then be obliged to recall governors, that is, order them back to England, or repeal laws the colonists objected to. Samuel Adams grew up thinking that protesting was a perfectly natural part of life for a colonist.

By making sure that just about everyone in Boston could read and write, colonists could help protect their rights. Almost all children went to a school of some sort. The girls and some boys went to dame schools taught by widows or spinsters in their homes. The children learned the alphabet, spelling, basic arithmetic, and how to make their letters. This is all the formal schooling most girls had. It was considered enough for them. Boys usually went on to grammar or writing schools where they learned a higher level of reading, writing, spelling, and arithmetic. Many boys were then apprenticed from age 13 until they were 21 to men who taught them a trade such as candlemaking, blacksmithing, printing, silversmithing, sail making, butchering, or other skills so they could earn a living.

The Adamses hoped their son would become a minister. At the age of seven Samuel started to go to the Boston Latin School on School Street. He was taught Latin and Greek, history and literature, geography and science. But to learn arithmetic, writing, and spelling, he had to go to a separate writing school. Much time at the Boston Latin School was devoted to the study of religion. To learn all this, schoolboys spent long hours six days a week seated on hard wooden benches listening, reciting, and studying. They had only Thursday and Saturday afternoons off. By the time he was 10, Samuel had memorized several books of Latin literature. His schoolmaster was Nathaniel Williams. As was a common practice at that time, he beat the boys with a stick called a ferule if they were late or did not know their lessons. But Adams was a model student and seldom felt the schoolmaster's rod.

In the fall of 1736, after Samuel turned 14, he left his comfortable home and crossed the Charles River to the town of Cambridge. There he took up residence at Harvard College. Samuel Adams was living away from home for the first time.

Twenty-two students were in Samuel's class. Each lived in a large room with several other young fellows. Their day started at six in the morning when the bell was rung for prayers. Breakfast was two large slices of bread and a mug of ale. Classes started at eight o'clock. Lunch at noon was more bread and ale. Lectures, studying, and reciting went on until prayers at five. Dinner was at seven-thirty. Students ate together in the Commons, a dining room in old Harvard Hall. They were served platters of bread and meat. The students almost rioted every night over the food because there was never enough. They usually had to buy or steal more food to satisfy their big appetites. At nine the bell was rung, and they went to bed. All day Saturday they studied religion, and all day Sunday they attended church.

Harvard was a Puritan college where no entertainments were allowed. The students were commanded to be sober, righteous, and godly at all times. But they were young boys, and they found it hard to always suppress their high spirits. They bedeviled the college president and their tutors with practical jokes and pranks whenever they could get away with it.

Young Adams got on well with his classmates and teachers. He was quiet, soft spoken, and friendly. Although his speaking voice was high and often squeaked when he talked, he had a good tenor singing voice and he loved to sing. Later in his life, he founded several singing societies in Boston. He grew to be medium height, but thin and pale, almost sickly-looking. It was his

Harvard College, Cambridge, Massachusetts, in 1739 at the time Samuel Adams was a student there.

intense dark blue eyes and his heavy eyebrows that people noticed most about him.

To prepare for the ministry, Samuel studied Hebrew, philosophy, and ethics. His preparation also included courses in divinity, which is theology, the study of religious faith, practice, and experience, especially the study of God and God's relation to the world. All this was in addition to more Greek, Latin, and physics and other sciences at that time called natural philosophy. Much emphasis was placed on rhetoric, the study and practice of writing and speaking effectively. Rhetoric began in ancient Greek and Roman times as the study of methods and rules of training public speakers to be informative and persuasive. It was one of Samuel's best subjects.

But Samuel also read the writings of political men from more modern times. The man whose ideas made the deepest impression on him was the great 17th-century English political philosopher John Locke. The execution of King Charles I of England by the Puritans in 1649 marked in England the beginning of the end of the idea that kings ruled by divine right. After 1688, monarchs in England no longer claimed to rule by divine right. Instead, the Parliament had gained much of the political power—particularly the lower house, the House of Commons, whose members were elected representatives. The upper house, the House of Lords, was made up of members of the nobility and bishops of the Church of England. After these drastic changes in Great Britain, Locke published several important books. He wrote that people should determine their own governments. According to Locke, all men should be considered politically equal and had three basic rights—life, liberty, and property. The role of government should be limited to protecting those rights. Locke stated that a government should not seize a person's property nor should it raise taxes without the consent of the people given through their elected representatives. Locke also wrote that people had the right to resist and overthrow tyrants. Samuel Adams thought a lot about Locke's writings while at Harvard. He came to adopt these ideals of equality and liberty as his own personal beliefs.

While still at a young, impressionable age, Samuel Adams adopted other beliefs that set the course of his life. In 1740, the year he graduated from Harvard, a religious movement known as the Great Awakening swept the New England colonies. George Whitefield, a young clergyman from England, preached to large outdoor crowds in Georgia, Philadelphia, and New England, transforming the people almost overnight. His powerful sermons about the horrors of hell and the joys of heaven swept up many of his listeners into a religious "new birth." With this message, Whitefield influenced many different Protestant groups. In Boston, his powerful preaching made the latter-day Puritans see they must return to the old-fashioned "pure" Puritanism of their grandparents. There were never any theaters or entertainments, like dances, in Boston, for they were considered works of the devil. But when Whitefield came and preached, even rich people gave up their fine clothes and returned to the simple black dresses and suits of the colony's Puritan founders.

Nowhere was the change more striking than at Harvard College. After the Reverend George Whitefield spoke there, the boys played no more pranks nor drank hard spirits. Instead, they prayed in their rooms, in their classes, and in the Commons.

This deep religious fervor, even frenzy, left a profound impression on young Adams. Although the return to Puritanism did not last among the general population, it remained with Samuel Adams for the rest of his life. He worked tirelessly to return at least Boston and Massachusetts to simple living—hard work, soberness, and strong religious faith. He thought money-making led to selfishness and a turning away from God. It made people soft and their determination weak.

Yet despite his deep religious beliefs, Adams realized that becoming a minister did not really interest him. His parents, especially his mother, were very disappointed, but they did not tell their son what to do. Since most of the political leaders Adams had read about were lawyers, he decided to study the law. He returned to Harvard in the fall of 1740 to begin work on his master's degree.

In the spring of 1741, the comfortable world of the Adamses collapsed. Deacon Adams faced total financial ruin. The Land Bank, which he had founded in 1740 and had put much of his own money into, had been outlawed by the British government in London. Deacon Adams faced prison, his family poverty.

There was little hard money, that is, gold and silver, in the colonies. The British government did not permit British coins to be minted outside Great Britain nor could gold and silver money be exported to the colonies. What little gold and silver there was in the colonies came from ships' captains who traded illegally with other countries, like Spain, France, and the Netherlands. With little cash money, the colonists had to barter, that is, to trade one product for another. In the southern colonies, tobacco served as currency. In New England, livestock and grain were bartered. Although Parliament had previously allowed Massachusetts to issue some paper money, in 1739 the governor had been ordered to take much of that out of circulation.

By 1740, the lack of currency had been so severe that a great depression occurred. Many people could not earn any money. They had their land seized for nonpayment of debts, and the people themselves were put into debtors' prison. Poor people faced the same kind of situation their ancestors had experienced centuries before in England. There they had been tenant farmers working on land rented from wealthy landlords generation after generation. This is what Deacon Adams's great-grandfather, Henry Adams, had been when he left England to come to the Massachusetts Bay Colony in 1638.

Deacon Adams and others saw the plight of the colonists and decided to form a land bank that would issue paper money to be used to buy things and pay off debts. Other colonies had done this to help people over hard times. However, banks must be backed up by money of some sort, usually gold and silver. Since there was very little, Deacon Adams and his friends put up their own lands to back the paper money.

But the royal governor and the wealthy merchants were against the Land Bank, saying it was inflationary. Prices would skyrocket and the paper money become worthless, they predicted. The most outspoken opponent of the Land Bank was an expert in financial matters and the wealthiest merchant in all the colonies, Thomas Hutchinson. He urged Governor Jonathan Belcher to send letters to England pleading with the British government to stop the bank.

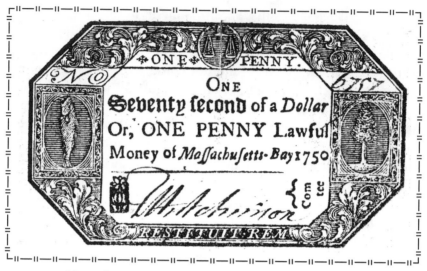

Massachusetts paper money printed nine years after the collapse of Deacon Adams's Land Bank.

The next year, word came that the British Parliament had declared the Land Bank illegal and had dissolved it. What was worse, the founders of the bank, like Deacon Adams, were made responsible for redeeming their bank's money, that is, giving gold and silver for all the paper money they had issued. If they could not, they would go to prison. The sheriff put notices in the newspaper saying Deacon Adams's house, gardens, brewery, wharf, and lands were to be sold at auction to pay these debts. But the Samuel Adamses—father and son—threatened to sue the sheriff for *his* property. This scared the sheriff enough for him to postpone the sale, and he kept postponing it.

Many people were so angry at the closing of the Land Bank that they threatened open rebellion. Farmers from all over Massachusetts planned a march on Boston. The governor stopped the protest by arresting the leaders and putting them in prison. The poor men of Boston knew whom to blame. A mob armed with clubs marched on Thomas Hutchinson's house. They broke windows so he could hear their curses. Then someone set the house on fire, and the crowd yelled, "Let it burn!"

The colonists' outrage caused the king to recall Governor

Jonathan Belcher and send another governor, William Shirley, in his place. Once the new governor came, the severe penalties against Deacon Adams were reduced, but he still lost a large part of his fortune. For all their troubles, young Samuel Adams held Thomas Hutchinson personally responsible.

During the worst of the crisis, Samuel wanted to leave college and go to work to help his family. But his father would not allow him to make this sacrifice. However, young Adams had to cut back on his expenses. Instead of living and eating at a comfortable boardinghouse outside the college grounds, he returned to live at Harvard. He became a waiter at the Commons so he could get his meals free.

When Samuel Adams received his master's degree in 1743, he wrote a paper titled "Whether it be lawful to resist the Supreme Magistrate if the Commonwealth cannot be otherwise preserved." This fancy language meant that Adams thought it was all right under certain circumstances for people to revolt against their government and rulers. This could be considered treason, for which he could have been jailed or even hanged. But no one paid any attention to what a young college boy proposed. College boys often said outrageous things.

Yet Samuel Adams knew exactly what he was saying. With the near rebellion of the common people over the Land Bank, he recognized the power of a mob to bring about change.

CHAPTER TWO

Clergy, Lawyer, Merchant, Chief?

After graduating from college and then earning his master's degree by the age of 21, Samuel Adams still did not know what he wanted to do with his life. Young Adams knew he did not want to become a minister. His mother did not want him to be a lawyer. About the only thing left for someone with his background was business.

His father secured a position for him in the countinghouse (an 18th-century accounting and business office) of his friend Thomas Cushing. Even with his fine education, Samuel Adams had to start in an entry-level position of clerk. All day he perched on a high stool with a quill pen in his hand, making endless entries into account ledgers. The work bored him to death. What he liked to do was talk politics with his fellow workers, especially his employer's son, young Thomas Cushing. Evenings he often stayed late in the taverns talking, which made him sleepy at work in the mornings. Sleepy countinghouse clerks made mistakes. Within a few months, Mr. Cushing went to Deacon Adams. As politely as he could, Cushing told Adams that his son would never make a merchant of himself. Young Samuel Adams lacked any business sense at all.

Deacon Adams thought perhaps his son was too well educated and too smart to work at a clerk's tasks. He decided to lend him £1,000 (about $4,500) so he could go into business for himself. At that time, £1,000 was a large sum of money equal to several years' earnings of an average craftsworker. Young Adams took in a partner and gave him half the money. Within six months the partner had lost the money, and Samuel Adams lost his half, too. In fact, he found himself in debt. Not knowing what else to do, Deacon Adams took his son into his own brewing business where he could supervise him. After all, Samuel would one day take over the business, so he might as well learn it.

But it was the same story as at Cushing's countinghouse. Young Adams had no interest in ale, rum, or molasses. He worked at his job because he had no choice. Dutifully, he went to his office every day and put in his hours. His father was very busy with his other business interests and his work as a representative in the Massachusetts General Court. He hoped his son would expand the business, run it more efficiently, come up with new ideas. But Samuel Adams, the younger, had no interest in making money.

Instead of attending to business, Samuel Adams liked to be out among all kinds of people. Most young men with his family background and excellent education would not associate with men of the "meaner sort"—poor people, unskilled laborers, indentured servants. But like his father before him, Adams treated everyone he met as an equal. In turn, the common people were honored to be noticed by this gentleman.

While Deacon Adams despaired of his son's lack of ambition, he welcomed him as a political ally. Young Adams had become very good at arguing politics. His father took him to meetings of the Caucus Club and introduced him to the men who really ran Boston. But it was not until 1746 that the Caucus Club nominated young Adams for an office. He was elected one of the clerks of Boston's three markets, a nonpaying political position. At each market, farmers brought their produce to sell and craftsworkers offered their goods. Adams's duties were to make sure the market opened and closed on time and to settle any differences of opinion between sellers and buyers.

That same year, Deacon Adams was nominated for membership to the governor's Council by the House of Representatives, the lower house of Massachusetts's lawmaking body, the General Court. This selection was a great honor because the Council was the upper house of the General Court. But Governor William Shirley had veto power over 13 of its 28 members, and he vetoed—refused to approve—Adams. The governor wanted only gentlemen of the "better sort" on the Council. Deacon Adams associated with common laborers in the Caucus Club. Besides, Adams had founded the Land Bank in opposition to the previous governor. His loyalty to royal governors could not be counted on.

19

The Adamses were crushed. Until now, they had thought William Shirley was a good governor. But his veto of the deacon was an insult to the family. The Adamses declared war on the governor. They organized political opposition to him and successfully prevented him from getting a raise in salary. They investigated his expenditures. They opposed everything he did, good and bad.

Young Samuel Adams, to annoy Governor Shirley, organized his own political club with his young friends. It had no name and membership was a deep secret. The main activity of the club was to publish a weekly four-page newspaper called the *Public Advertizer*, which constantly ran articles jabbing at Governor Shirley.

But most of the people of the Massachusetts colony supported Shirley because in the mid-1740s there was a war on. Great Britain was involved in one of a series of wars with France. French troops from what is now Canada, along with their Native American allies, were harassing the northern borders of the New England colonies as well as Great Britain's colony in Nova Scotia. There were few regular British troops in North America. The colonists had to depend on their own militias for defense. Governor Shirley managed to persuade seven of the other colonies to send troops to join the militias of Massachusetts to fight against the French. In 1745, instead of waiting for the French to attack them, the militias captured the French fortress of Louisbourg on Cape Breton Island. It was a glorious victory, and the people of Boston celebrated for days.

Governor Shirley demanded that the king repay the royal Province of Massachusetts for this great victory. Several months later, a ship arrived in Boston loaded with £200,000 of gold, silver, and copper coins. Hard money at last. Almost everybody prospered, including the Adamses and their brewery.

Yet Samuel Adams and his friends in their *Public Advertizer* found fault even with this. Adams opposed too much civil and military power being in one man's hands. He criticized the governor for the prosperity because, he claimed, it was causing a decline in such Puritan virtues as thrift, hard work, and strictness in matters of religion and conduct. But the people had no interest in giving up the good life to return to penny-pinching Puritanism. The *Public Advertizer* went out of business in a year. Nevertheless, Samuel Adams had shown himself to be a good political writer.

Any hope young Adams had for a political career seemed to come to an end when his father died suddenly on March 8, 1748 at the age of 59. Samuel was left to care for his widowed mother and the large brewing business. The next year he added to his responsibilities by marrying. On October 17, 1749, Samuel Adams wedded Elizabeth "Betty" Checkley, a distant relative and the daughter of the minister who had baptized him. The young couple went to live in the house on Purchase Street.

Over the next few years, the Adamses saw a decline in their income because Samuel Adams would not tend to the brewery business. He wrote, "But I get out of my Line when I touch upon Commerce, it is a Subject I never understood." His political career suffered without his father's help. He had never proved himself in business nor anything else, so people had no reason to respect his abilities. Not until 1753 was he elected to a town office again—as scavenger, or commissioner of garbage collection. Finally, in 1756, he was elected one of five tax collectors for the town of Boston. This, at least, brought in a steady salary of £100 a year. But the next year brought tragedy to his life. On July 25, his wife died at the age of 32, a few weeks after giving birth to their fifth child. Samuel Adams was left with two surviving children— Hannah and Samuel—to raise by himself. Soon after losing his wife, he faced the loss of his home.

While Adams was reading the August 4, 1758, edition of the *Boston News-Letter*, he saw something that caused him to bolt out of his chair. An advertisement had been placed there by Sheriff Stephen Greenleaf. It read: "To be sold at public Auction at the Exchange Tavern in Boston, To-morrow at noon. The Dwelling House, Malt-House, and other buildings, with the Garden and lands adjoining, and the Wharf, Dock and Flats before the same, being part of the estate of the late *Samuel Adams*, Esq., deceased. . . for the more speedy finishing of the Land-Bank, or Manufactory schemes." This was the fourth time the town officials and the Land Bank commissioners had tried to put up the Adams properties for sale. Samuel Adams took up his pen and started writing.

In the next edition of the *Boston News-Letter* appeared an open letter saying that the previous sheriff had been "advised by gentlemen of the law, that his proceedings was illegal and unwarrantable." Adams then went on to threaten to bring a countersuit against the present sheriff and his property. To scare off any prospective buyers, he said he would prosecute anyone who trespassed on his estate. The auction was postponed indefinitely.

While Samuel Adams was confronting his personal financial problems, Great Britain was dealing with serious military problems. The French in Canada and the British along the American coast of the Atlantic Ocean had been fighting each other off and on since 1689. Most of these wars had been over the fur trade or fishing rights or religion or were the result of wars going on in Europe. What was to be their final battle in North America broke out in 1754. The French and Indian War was sparked by a young colonel in the Virginia militia named George Washington. On orders from the Virginia governor, he led a small band of troops to force the French to withdraw from the Ohio Valley, which both France and Great Britain claimed. He was badly defeated.

At the same time as Washington's ill-fated expedition, seven colonies—Massachusetts, New York, Connecticut, Rhode Island, Pennsylvania, Maryland, and New Hampshire—sent representatives to a meeting that planned a union among most of the North American colonies for their common defense against attacks by the French and France's Native American allies. But the plan was not approved by the colonial assemblies or by Great Britain. Nevertheless, Great Britain did send professional troops from England to fight beside the colonists. But once the regulars came, they discriminated against the colonials. The colonial soldiers did not receive as much pay, and they were not allowed to wear the British red uniforms. This set up differences between supposedly equal Englishmen. The colonial militiamen did not forget these incidents when they returned to their homes after the war.

The fighting was over in North America after the British captured Quebec in 1759 and Montreal in 1760. In the Treaty of Paris signed in 1763, France lost all its territory on the North American

In 1754, Benjamin Franklin created this cartoon and slogan to promote a union of the colonies for their common defense.

continent except two islands off Canada and two islands in the Caribbean. Great Britain got Canada and all the land from the Appalachian Mountains to the Mississippi River, plus Florida. In late 1762, France had given New Orleans and the land west of the Mississippi River to its ally Spain. That was to compensate Spain for its loss of Florida to the British.

Now what was Great Britain to do with this vast North American territory? The British government wanted to keep a standing army of at least 10,000 soldiers to man former French forts along the Mississippi River, as well as at Fort Detroit, Fort Niagara, Montreal, and Quebec. The colonies were reluctant to supply that many men. Standing armies cost a great deal of money. Great Britain already had huge war debts, and its people were paying heavy taxes. Now it also had to find some way to pay for this large army.

Between 1607 and 1733 Great Britain had founded 13 colonies on the North American continent from Massachusetts

British troops at the Battle of Quebec. After winning the war, Britain wanted to station 10,000 troops in North America.

Bay in the north to the Georgia colony in the south. Several of these colonies, such as Virginia and Massachusetts Bay, had been established by businessmen in Great Britain who formed private trading companies. Other colonies, such as Maryland and Pennsylvania, were run by proprietors, individuals to whom the kings of England, starting with James I, had granted millions of acres of land in North America. The trading companies' and proprietors' plan was to make money by having people settle these lands. The settlers, or colonists, would then ship back to England items such as tobacco, fish, naval stores (pitch, tar, turpentine) and raw materials like timber and iron ore. England would send back to the colonies manufactured goods, like china, furniture, and cloth, and sell them to the settlers. It was a grand plan for making money, especially for the proprietors and for the merchants who had started the companies back in England.

To attract settlers, the companies and proprietors promised

them free or cheap land. What is more, these settlers or colonists could be quite free of royal control once they reached North America. They did not have to pay taxes to England. They could decide themselves what taxes would be needed to pay for their local schools, roads, and other town expenses. Many oppressive British laws did not apply to them. Their colonial assemblies could pass their own laws. In a few of the colonies, most people could even worship as they pleased. As long as they traded only with Great Britain, the king and the British Parliament did not much care what they did.

As new monarchs ruled Great Britain, the colonies got new charters. They became royal colonies no longer controlled by companies or proprietors. Massachusetts received its royal charter in 1691. But the colonists made sure they kept their special freedoms and privileges in the new charters. As the years passed, the colonists found they liked this arrangement. They came to strongly protest any controls their so-called mother country tried to place on them. In the midst of the French and Indian War, for example, many of the colonial assemblies refused to supply the British with the troops and money needed to fight the French. During the 18th century, many North American colonists even began to think of themselves as different from the people in Great Britain. They began calling themselves Americans.

With the end of the French and Indian War, all that intentional neglect on the part of Great Britain was about to change. If 10,000 men were to be kept in North America to protect the colonies, then the colonies were going to have to pay for them.

CHAPTER THREE

Samuel Adams, Political Activist

Twenty years had passed since Samuel Adams had graduated from Harvard with so much promise. By this time, his college classmates had become successful lawyers, merchants, and clergymen. They could not help but think Samuel Adams was strange. He had made nothing of himself. He had even thrown away his inheritance. Samuel Adams seemed to take pride in becoming poorer and poorer. The sea had reclaimed most of Adams Wharf where sailing ships once had berthed. He had let the fine house on Purchase Street deteriorate to the point where the neighbors patched it up so the roof would not leak on the Adams children. Grandmother Mary Adams fed and dressed Hannah and Samuel and saw that they went to school.

Few understood that for a very long time Samuel Adams had a self-appointed mission in life. He had succeeded his father as guardian of the rights and liberties granted in the Massachusetts colony's 1691 charter. Unlike his father, the guarding of these principles had become both his profession and his consuming passion. He wrote, "we are the Descendents of Ancestors remarkeable for their Zeal for true Religion & Liberty." Everything else was secondary—family, food, clothing, financial security.

Over the years, Samuel Adams had come to know the people of Boston—the meaner sort, the middling sort, the better sort—as probably no other man did. He was as equally at home with day laborers as with Harvard men. In fact, he seemed to prefer the company he found in the tough waterfront taverns with names like Noah's Ark, Anchor Tavern, and Ship in Distress. The customers there were sailors, dockworkers, and even petty criminals. Adams would go to the shipyards at noontime and perch himself on a piling. While the workers ate their lunch, he talked to them about how they needed to guard the liberties granted them in the charter so their children could have a better life. No

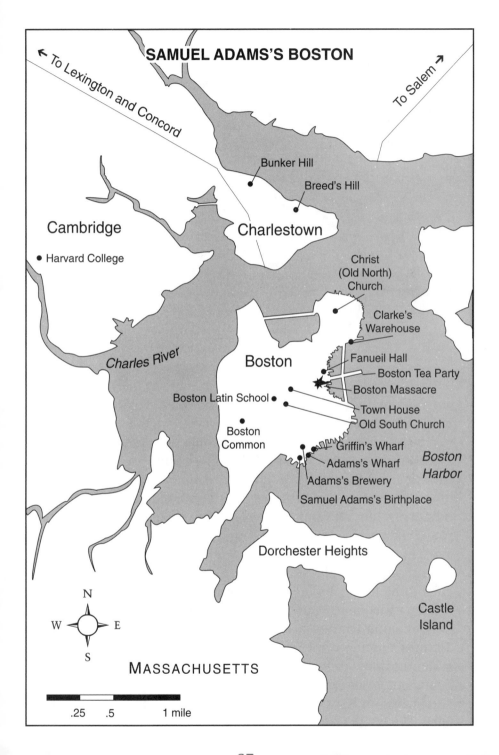

SAMUEL ADAMS'S BOSTON

To Lexington and Concord

To Salem

Bunker Hill

Breed's Hill

Cambridge

Charlestown

Harvard College

Christ
(Old North)
Church

Clarke's
Warehouse

Charles River

Boston

Fanueil Hall

Boston Tea Party

Boston Massacre

Boston Latin School

Town House

Old South Church

Boston
Common

Griffin's Wharf

Adams's Wharf

Boston
Harbor

Adams's Brewery

Samuel Adams's Birthplace

Dorchester Heights

N

W   E

S

Castle
Island

MASSACHUSETTS

.25   .5   1 mile

27

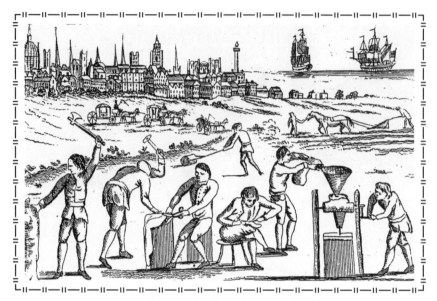

Boston artisans. Samuel Adams spent much of his time talking politics with Boston's skilled workers and day laborers.

such opportunities existed in England itself. His own poverty caused them to feel he was more on a level with them. They came to consider him their friend. Some people saw Samuel Adams as an eccentric but kindly man. He became a familiar sight, walking the streets of Boston wrapped in his shabby red cloak and followed everywhere by his huge Newfoundland dog, Queue. But others saw him as a sinister creature who lurked in the dark taprooms of taverns, always staying in the shadows, whispering while his friends did his bidding.

Although he had lost the respect of many of his peers, he had gained the friendship of other important gentlemen of Boston. The first was James Otis Junior, the brilliant lawyer. Adams and Otis became friends because they had a common enemy—Thomas Hutchinson. For a long time Adams had ranted against Hutchinson's grab for power. In 1758, Hutchinson had become lieutenant governor of the Province of Massachusetts Bay as the Massachusetts Bay Colony was officially known after 1691. By the early 1760s, he was also president of the Council, the upper house of the Massachusetts General Court, and captain of Castle Island—the fortress that guarded Boston Harbor. These were only his major offices. Hutchinson's relatives and friends held positions in the courts and government departments. For example, Andrew Oliver, his brother-in-law, was secretary of the province. As if all this had not been enough, in 1760 Hutchinson had seized the job of chief justice of the Superior Court from James Otis Senior. Both Governor Francis Bernard and Governor William Shirley before him had promised the job would go to Otis once it became vacant. James Otis Senior was one of the finest lawyers in the colony, with years of service to the governors and the king. Hutchinson was not even a lawyer. Because of this insult, James Otis Junior became Hutchinson's sworn enemy.

Samuel Adams knew just how James Otis Junior felt, and the two men became allies. In 1761, James Otis Junior was elected to the House of Representatives. He was reelected almost every year and became one of its leaders. Otis introduced and got legislation passed in his fiery speeches, which Samuel Adams "suggested." Adams also "edited" Otis's writings for the newspapers.

James Otis Jr. in 1761 being cheered by his supporters. Samuel Adams worked very closely with Otis.

Adams began to look to Harvard College for recruits to his cause of defending the charter. He was especially interested in the Harvard graduates because they had read the writings of John Locke and the ancient Greeks and Romans as he had. His second cousin John Adams was the most brilliant. Although very different from Samuel, John Adams understood his cousin's ideas, and together they became known as "that brace [pair] of Adamses."

Another Harvard recruit was a most unlikely one—John Hancock. Hancock at the age of 27 had inherited £70,000 from his wealthy uncle. Because he was the richest man in the colony second only to Thomas Hutchinson, many expected that he would be a strong supporter of the governor and the king. It was Samuel Adams who recognized this young man had greatness in him. It puzzled many people that two such different men would take up the same cause. But in reality, they were the product of the same experiences. Both had read the works of the ancient Greek and Roman philosophers and statesmen, and those of John Locke. Both had strong religious upbringings. While Hancock reveled in his wealth, Adams reveled in his poverty.

As a pious man, Adams was welcome among ministers. He attended church every Sunday, said prayers, and read the Bible with his children daily. Although he had little money, he gave more than he could afford to his church. He organized some of the ministers into an influential political group called the "Black Regiment" for the somber, dark clothing they wore as a mark of their profession. From the beginning of the Massachusetts colony, the Puritan clergy had been political leaders as well as moral and religious leaders. They considered it their duty to tell the members of their churches what to do and think in every area of their lives. In their long Sunday sermons, the ministers had great opportunities to harangue their captive audience against acts of the British government. Adams did not,

John Adams, one of Samuel's cousins, was also a Harvard graduate.

of course, dictate what they should say. His way was to suggest with great logic. No one could deny his logic that Parliament had no right to interfere with the rights in the charter granted by the king. This was his whole argument—for a while.

Adams's only income was from his job as a tax collector. But he would not or could not keep books despite his education in higher mathematics and his brief experience at Cushing's countinghouse. He was so sympathetic that he did not press people to pay the taxes they owed, especially after the end of the French and Indian War. There was a serious depression, and people could not afford to pay. When the colony's treasury found itself unusually short of money, an investigation of the tax collectors was launched. All were found to be short, but Adams was short the most—£7,000. Hutchinson charged him with malfeasance in office, meaning he thought Adams had embezzled, or stolen, the money. He tried to put Adams on trial. In March 1764, Samuel Adams stood before the town meeting and admitted he was short in his tax account. He refused to run for office again. But he had made himself so popular among the taxpayers that he was reelected anyway on his promise to try to do a better job.

Town meetings were the way in which the Massachusetts colony governed itself at the local level. As often as necessary, in every town, the men who owned property—men such as ministers, doctors, lawyers, and farmers—met and decided among themselves what needed to be done. Everyone was entitled to give his opinion and be listened to. But common people who owned no property—people like servants, clerks, and day laborers—could not vote at town meetings. Nor could women, Jews, Catholics, or free Blacks and Native Americans vote, no matter how much property they owned. The town meeting elected local officials and delegates to the Massachusetts House of Representatives. The representatives were then given a list of instructions on how they were to vote. If new issues came up, another town meeting was called and new instructions were given to the representatives. According to the charter, there had to be at least one town meeting a year.

Boston town meetings were held in Faneuil Hall, a public market and meeting place. In 1764 and 1765, there was serious

Samuel Adams opposed the Revenue Act of 1764, which placed taxes on certain goods imported into the colonies.

business before the town, and Samuel Adams knew more about it than anyone else. At last what he had been talking and writing about to the people of Boston for years had come to pass. The liberties of the people and the rights granted in the charters were being threatened as never before. The British Parliament was about to tax the colonies to pay for the 10,000 soldiers stationed in North America. But nowhere in the colonies' royal charters did it say Parliament was allowed to tax the colonies. Before the town meeting, Adams argued that he really did not see why the colonies needed soldiers now that the war was over. The colonies had always protected themselves, and they would continue to do so. The Americans had a fear of standing armies. In Europe, armies had always meant tyranny over the people. Although he was officially only a tax collector and a few times moderator of the Boston town meeting, Adams appointed himself chief opponent of any taxes Parliament might pass.

But Samuel Adams always liked to remain in the background. When Parliament passed the Revenue Act of 1764 known as the Sugar Act, Adams had no problems persuading his fiery friend, James Otis Junior, to lead the protest against the new taxes. The Sugar Act actually lowered the tax on molasses but put import duties or taxes on cloth, wines, coffee, and other items. Otis wrote and published a pamphlet entitled *The Rights of the British Colonies Asserted and Proved.* Otis stated, "Taxes are not to be laid on the people but by their consent in person or by deputation [representation]." The idea quickly became the rallying cry, "Taxation without representation is tyranny."

Despite Adams's and Otis's railing against the Sugar Act, they could not get the support of the people. The people did not see it affecting them much. Merchants and sea captains continued to smuggle molasses and just added cloth, wines, and coffee to their cargoes. The customs commissioners whose job it was to collect the sugar tax continued to accept bribes and look the other way.

On December 6,1764, Adams married 24-year-old Elizabeth "Betsy" Wells, one of the prettiest young women in the colony. She was the daughter of merchant Francis Wells, who, unlike most parents of the time, believed in more education for girls. Betsy Wells probably came closer to Samuel Adams in education than any other woman in the colony. Why she accepted Adams, who was twice her age, prematurely gray, stooped, and by this time suffering from an inherited shaking illness, was a mystery to all. What is more, he faced possible trial and imprisonment for tax embezzlement. But marry him she did, and she became his strongest supporter. She loved his children, fixed up his house, and made it possible for him to fulfill his destiny.

CHAPTER FOUR

The Sons of Liberty

The year 1765 was a bad one. In January, Harvard College burned. In February, the dreaded disease smallpox swept over Boston. In April, word reached Boston that a Stamp Act had been passed in Parliament. It was to take effect on November 1.

Great Britain's new prime minister, George Grenville, believed that surely the stamp tax would be a fair way to raise part of the money to pay for the military expenses. The stamp tax was not an import tax. It would be the first ever British-imposed tax within the colonies. The stamp tax would be a tax affecting everyone. Stamps would be required on every legal transaction—on documents such as rental leases, apprenticeship papers, mortgages, land deeds, liquor licenses, marriage licenses—and on all sorts of other items such as playing cards, dice, diplomas, even pamphlets, books, and newspapers. The stamps would cost from a half penny on a newspaper to £10 for lawyers to be permitted to practice law before the courts. What is more, the stamps had to be paid for in hard money—gold and silver. Colonists feared that this would soon drain all the cash money from the colonies again. It seemed to many colonists that this was 1740 all over again. The law stated that the money raised by the tax was to be spent in the colonies and only for the purpose of "defending, protecting and securing the British colonies." Nevertheless, how the money would be spent would not be under the control of colonial legislatures.

Naturally the stamp tax would especially hurt the merchants, lawyers, shipowners, journalists, and clergy, whose activities required the special stamps. But since it also affected so many activities of ordinary people, it gave everyone a reason to complain. It united people. It even began to unite the colonies.

Virginia, the first of the 13 colonies, was also the first to protest the Stamp Act. On May 29, 1765, Patrick Henry, a young lawyer and delegate to Virginia's lawmaking body, the House of Burgesses, made a fiery speech against the Stamp Act. He finished the speech with words that became immortal. "Tarquin and Caesar had each his Brutus; Charles the First, his Cromwell; and George the Third [At this point, some listeners shouted, "Treason! Treason!"] may profit from their example. If this be treason, make the most of it." In the House of Burgesses, Patrick

A British tax stamp. Adams opposed the Stamp Act of 1765, which was supposed to raise £60,000 a year in the colonies.

Henry proposed seven resolutions against the Stamp Act. The resolutions declared the Stamp Act illegal, unconstitutional, and unjust. They said the British had no right to impose internal taxes upon the colonies. Virginians were entitled to all the rights held by the people of Great Britain. The House of Burgesses adopted four of the less radical resolutions, which were called the Virginia Resolves. But all seven of the Resolves were sent to all the colonies. Some said the Virginia Resolves were treasonous. Others came to respect and honor the brave Virginians.

Samuel Adams began exchanging letters with Patrick Henry. He drew up his own list of Massachusetts Resolves, which James Otis saw were passed by the Massachusetts House of Representatives. Otis went a step further and invited all the colonies to send delegates to a general congress. They would meet in New York City on October 7, 1765, to plan a united resistance to the Stamp Act. Nine out of the 13 colonies accepted.

But October was a long way from June, and people could not wait. Boston merchants agreed not to import any English goods until the Stamp Act was repealed. In fact, it may have been Adams who whispered the idea in their ears in the first place. He knew that this would deal a heavy blow to English businesses and cut down on the amount of taxes the British government could collect. But he had another reason. The boycott would prevent the people from buying any "fripperies" and "baubles," as he called luxury English products. They would be forced to return to simple Puritanism.

Not everyone in the British Parliament supported the Stamp Act either. One of the strongest speeches against it came from Colonel Isaac Barré, a member of Parliament who was a veteran of the French and Indian War. He praised the colonial settlers, calling them "Sons of Liberty." The whole speech was published in the colonies.

Samuel Adams quickly adopted the Sons of Liberty name. He formed a semisecret Sons of Liberty society in Boston made up of laborers, craftsmen, artisans, and some wealthy, educated gentlemen. No lists of names were kept, so only members knew who belonged—and who did not. It was controlled by the leaders of the Caucus Club, a group of men calling themselves the Loyal

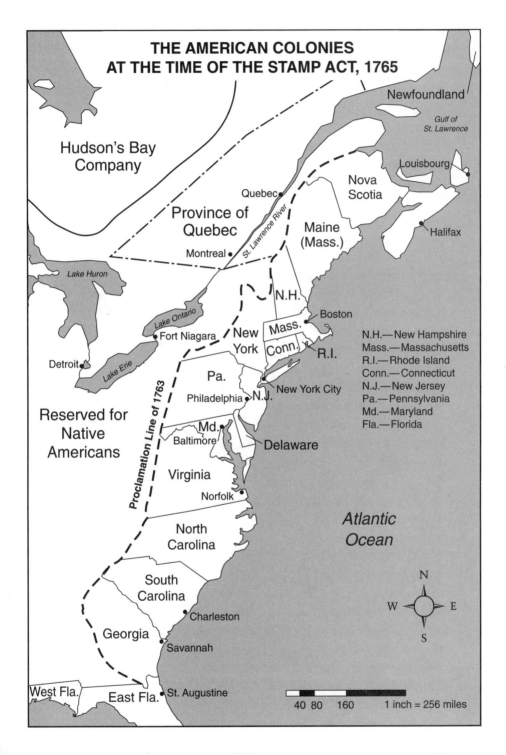

THE AMERICAN COLONIES
AT THE TIME OF THE STAMP ACT, 1765

Newfoundland

Gulf of
St. Lawrence

Hudson's Bay
Company

Louisbourg

Nova
Scotia

Quebec

Province of
Quebec

St. Lawrence River

Maine
(Mass.)

Halifax

Montreal

Lake Huron

N.H.

Boston

Lake Ontario

Fort Niagara

New
York

Mass.

Conn.

R.I.

Detroit

Lake Erie

N.H.—New Hampshire
Mass.—Massachusetts
R.I.—Rhode Island
Conn.—Connecticut
N.J.—New Jersey
Pa.—Pennsylvania
Md.—Maryland
Fla.—Florida

Pa.

New York City

Philadelphia

N.J.

Reserved for
Native
Americans

Proclamation Line of 1763

Md.

Baltimore

Delaware

Virginia

Norfolk

Atlantic
Ocean

North
Carolina

South
Carolina

Charleston

N

Georgia

Savannah

W   E

S

West Fla.

East Fla.

St. Augustine

40 80   160   1 inch = 256 miles

Nine. Neither Adams nor Otis was one of them, but Adams was their main adviser.

The Loyal Nine were, in turn, controlled by the men of the Long Room Club. They met from 1762 on in a room above the print shop where the *Boston Gazette* newspaper was published. This newspaper was the voice of Samuel Adams where for many years he had published open letters warning the people to take care of their liberties. Adams belonged to the Long Room Club, as did Otis and Hancock. Also invited to join these gentlemen was a

Portrait of Paul Revere painted by John Singleton Copley. Along with Adams, Revere belonged to the Long Room Club.

trusted artisan, the silversmith Paul Revere. There were only 16 members, 11 of them were graduates of Harvard College.

Samuel Adams gave the people symbols to rally around. He designated a giant elm tree in Boston's Hanover Square as the Liberty Tree, and he proclaimed the area under its widespread branches Liberty Hall. Soon Sons of Liberty organizations cropped up in all the colonies, in large towns and tiny hamlets. In Charleston, South Carolina, the Sons of Liberty came from the Firemen's Association. In Philadelphia, Pennsylvania, the Heart and Hand Fire Company began calling themselves the Sons of Liberty. Some groups did not call themselves by that name but "Committee of Safety" or "True Born Whigs." (The Whig Party was a political party in Great Britain. One part of it supported the colonists in their opposition to the Stamp Act.) Almost every community soon had a Liberty Tree of its own.

On the morning of August 14, 1765, early risers passing through Hanover Square could not help but notice two unusual things hanging in the Liberty Tree. One was an effigy, or dummy, of a man everyone recognized as Andrew Oliver—secretary of the Province of Massachusetts Bay and kinsman of Thomas Hutchinson. Oliver had also been given the new job of stamp master under the Stamp Act. The other thing hanging in the tree was a large boot with a puppet dressed as the devil peeking out of it. This was supposed to represent Lord Bute, who the colonists believed had introduced the Stamp Act in Parliament. Shops closed, and all work stopped as people came to look at the tree.

Governor Francis Bernard was outraged and called a meeting of the Council at the Town House. Lieutenant Governor Hutchinson ordered Sheriff Stephen Greenleaf to remove the effigies. By the time the sheriff and his few constables got to the Liberty Tree, several thousand people had gathered. The sheriff quickly recognized he would start trouble if he tried to remove the effigies. He retreated and the figures hung in the tree all day.

At dusk, the Sons of Liberty cut the dummies down and laid them on a platform. They then formed a procession of several hundred men. The solemn group moved slowly toward the Town House where the Council was still meeting. As they passed beneath the open windows, they chanted, "Liberty, property—

Bostonians reading about the Stamp Act. Lawyers, tavern keepers, shipowners, and publishers were particularly upset.

and no stamps." It was Adams's idea to chant this paraphrase of John Locke's "Life, liberty and property." All remained quiet and orderly until the group reached a building someone told them Andrew Oliver planned to use as the new stamp office. The men tore the building apart and built a huge bonfire with the lumber and the effigies.

The once orderly protesters were out of control. Oliver's house was nearby. The mob headed for it. They broke down the front door with axes. Once inside, they demolished furniture, smashed mirrors and windows. Most headed for the wine cellar. Oliver and his family were trapped on the second floor. Desperate to save them, Oliver promised the mob to resign as stamp master. The next morning, Oliver stood beneath the Liberty Tree and repeated his pledge. He was applauded and cheered by Bostonians. For years afterward in New England, August 14 was celebrated as a holiday. The people felt they had awakened the spirit of liberty across North America that day.

Sons of Liberty stormed the forts at Charleston and New York, too. Just as in Boston, every stamp master in every colony was forced to resign his office. In one colony, the Sons of Liberty kidnapped the stamp master, put him in an open grave, and threatened to bury him alive if he did not resign. However, in 1765 liberty did not mean independence from Great Britain. Liberty to the colonists meant those rights granted in their charters and guaranteed to all Englishmen.

Actually, Secretary Oliver, Governor Bernard, and Lieutenant Governor Hutchinson were against the Stamp Act, too. Hutchinson had written and spoken publicly against it. Everyone knew that. But Otis and Adams wanted to get rid of Hutchinson so they started a whispering campaign of rumors that Hutchinson had actually proposed the Stamp Act to Parliament. Some of the "meaner sort" probably did not know what the Stamp Act really meant. They only knew that they were going to be taxed more, even though they lacked jobs and money to support their families because of the economic depression. When their friend Samuel Adams told them Hutchinson and Parliament were to blame for their problems, they were ready to believe him.

Boston was used to mobs such as the one that attacked Oliver's house. There was a North End gang and a South End gang who hated each other. Every year on November 5, which was called Pope's Day, each gang built a huge float. On each float was placed a figure representing the pope surrounded by puppets dressed as devils. It showed the strong anti-Catholic feelings among the Puritans. The wagons were huge—20 to 40 feet long. As they were pulled through the streets by men and boys, people threw coins at them or gave the paraders food or rum. The whole day and night was like Halloween, complete with treats or tricks. People stole barrels, tore down fences, and gathered whatever else was not nailed down.

When the North and South gangs met, they would fight a ferocious battle to capture each other's floats. They used clubs, stones, and fists. Every year, men were badly hurt and a few even killed as the fight raged through the narrow streets. People either joined in or barricaded themselves in their houses. When one gang had won over the other, they marched outside Boston itself, built a bonfire, and burned both wagons. It was what they called a yearly "frolic."

On the night of August 26, 1765, a group of boys and former slaves (at that time about 1 in 12 Bostonians was an African American, either free or enslaved) built a fire in front of the Town House where the General Court met. It was an odd thing to do because the weather was so hot. The fire quickly attracted a crowd that would rather be outside than inside their homes on such a stifling night. Soon the sound of conch shells, whistles, and beating of drums was heard as a signal for men to come out and join the mob for a "frolic." The "frolic" was to attack Judge William Story's house. He was a member of the hated Admiralty Court, which had been set up to combat smuggling and would soon handle Stamp Act cases. The mob broke in, destroyed all of the official records and carried off the contents of his wine cellar.

Bostonians rioted and set bonfires in protest against the Stamp Act.

Then they went after Benjamin Hallowell's house. Hallowell was a customs commissioner who collected duties, or taxes, on imported goods. But those two men's misfortune was the warm-up for the big event—an attack on Lieutenant Governor Thomas Hutchinson's mansion.

Axes splintered the great front door as the family escaped out the back. The mob poured in and destroyed most of the house. Hutchinson had rare and valuable papers from which he was writing the history of Massachusetts. But the mob threw them in the gutter. They burned his many books. They tore down the woodwork, broke the furniture, and hammered holes in the walls. Then they went out and chopped down every tree in the garden, pulled up the flowers, and tore apart the bushes. Jewelry, silver, money, and clothing were stolen. The rioting went on until just before daylight when the mob finally faded away, its members fearing that they might be recognized.

The next morning the gentler citizens of Boston were shaken and frightened by this terrible, senseless destruction. A town meeting was hastily called in Fanueil Hall. It was the largest town meeting ever. The people voted their absolute disapproval of what had happened. But some of those who bewailed the dastardly deed the loudest were people whom Hutchinson recognized as having been in the mob.

Samuel Adams, however, was one of those genuinely shocked—and worried. He feared Hutchinson would win the town's sympathy and become a martyr. To prevent this, Adams circulated a rumor that letters had been found at Hutchinson's house proving that Hutchinson was responsible for the Stamp Act. But Adams never produced the letters. Adams also feared the mob had gone too far because Governor Bernard had been forced to flee to Castle Island in Boston Harbor. He might appeal for British troops to be sent to restore order. The only other police force was a sheriff and fewer than a dozen constables.

For the many crimes against Thomas Hutchinson's property, only one man was arrested, a shoemaker named Alexander MacKintosh, leader of the South End gang. But he was quickly released because of pressure on the sheriff from the Sons of Liberty before he could tell who ordered the riot.

Adams went to work organizing a letter-writing campaign to important people in London. They must be told that the destruction of Hutchinson's house was the work of outsiders, criminals in the town, and that the townspeople themselves were completely innocent of this outrage. Important people in the British government had to believe this so that troops would not be sent.

Although evidence points to the fact that Adams and others from the Long Room Club masterminded the demonstration of August 14, the Sons of Liberty had no part in the events of August

26 when Hutchinson's house was destroyed. But Adams knew the mob must not get out of hand again. They had to have discipline. A list had been discovered naming 15 gentlemen whose houses the mob was planning to plunder next. These gentlemen had nothing to do with the Stamp Act. The mob was using that excuse as a license to steal. Patriotism was not their motive.

Samuel Adams set about getting control of the North and South End gangs behind the mobs. It would not be easy, since they hated each other. First, he arranged for MacKintosh to get a job as a minor official. Then, he had him fitted out with a fine uniform and made him a general of his "troops," saying he expected them to be a second militia. The head of the North End mob and one of Adams's friends, was a man named Swift. He was a successful Harvard graduate who just liked fights. Adams appealed to his patriotism. No uniform and phony titles would fool him. Adams got the two sides to come together along with some important merchants and politicians at a huge banquet called a Union Feast. John Hancock paid for the whole party. Then on Pope's Day, there was a military-style parade in the streets of Boston with MacKintosh leading his "troops." But there was no fighting, looting, or destruction. There was no more mob action unless Samuel Adams ordered it.

In September 1765, a member of the House of Representatives from Boston died. The town meeting elected Samuel Adams to take his place. Although he would receive no pay, he would have some official power. Adams was sworn in on September 27, a few minutes before Governor Francis Bernard recessed the Massachusetts House of Representatives for its nonacceptance of the Stamp Act. This dismissal meant no laws or other legislative business could be carried on until the governor called them back.

On November 1, the day the Stamp Act was to take effect, all business stopped as if someone important had died. The Sons of Liberty hung an effigy of George Grenville, the prime minister of Great Britain, in the Liberty Tree. Later, they took it to the town gallows and "hanged" it to the cheers of thousands of Bostonians. The stamps were locked up in the fortress on Castle Island so that the Sons of Liberty could not seize them. None were to be had even if the people had been willing to pay for them.

affix the STAMP.

This is the Place to

Newspapers made fun of the tax stamp by printing skulls and crossbones.

Within a day or two, the newspapers were the first to break the stamp tax law. They printed a skull and crossbones where the hated stamp should have gone. By the middle of December, word reached Massachusetts that other colonies were resuming business as usual, without the stamps. Ships sailed, businesses opened, and judges of some of the courts heard cases.

On Friday May 16, 1766, the ship *Harrison*, six weeks out of England, dropped anchor in Boston Harbor. It carried the news that the new British prime minister, Lord Rockingham, who had taken power in July 1765, had led Parliament to repeal the Stamp Act in March 1766. As Samuel Adams had hoped, panic-stricken British merchants had pressed Parliament for repeal of the Stamp Act. Their businesses had been badly hurt by a sharp decrease in orders from the colonies. On Monday, May 19, Boston scheduled a huge celebration. At one in the morning, the first of the church bells began ringing. At two, the cannons on Castle Island boomed a salute. At dawn, the ships in the harbor fired their guns. By this time, the whole town was up and out to find the Liberty Tree decorated with ribbons and banners to its topmost branches. Musicians strolled the streets playing.

By nightfall, homes and shops in Boston had candles burning in every window. People redecorated the Liberty Tree with hundreds of lanterns. Over on the Boston Common, John Hancock's servants handed out pewter mugs filled with fine wine to make sure everyone had a good time. The people remembered him for it. Fireworks filled the sky out over the harbor. People were so happy that they collected money in order that the debtors could get out of prison.

What Samuel Adams did on this day of his triumph is not recorded. He did suggest that Massachusetts send letters of thanks to the king and Parliament with statements such as this:

> This is a repeated and striking instance of our most gracious Sovereign's [king's] paternal [fatherly] regard for the happiness and welfare of all his subjects. We feel upon this occasion, the deepest sense of loyalty and gratitude. We are abundantly convinced that our legal and constitutional rights and liberties will always be safe under his propitious [favorable] government. We esteem the relation we have ever stood in with Great Britain, the mother country, our happiness and security.

The other colonies sent similar letters of thanks.
But to his friends, Adams wrote,

> What a Blessing to us had the Stamp Act eventually . . . provd, which was calculated to enslave & ruin us. . . . When the Colonys saw the common Danger they at the same time saw their mutual Dependence & naturally calld in the Assistance of each other.

Adams knew this victory was not the end of the struggle. For with the repeal of the Stamp Act, Parliament had also passed the Declaratory Act, setting itself supreme over the colonies in order to bind the colonies and the people of America "in all cases whatsoever." This vague but clever wording did not mention taxes, but it certainly meant that Parliament still had the right to tax and regulate the colonies.

CHAPTER FIVE

Blood in the Snow

Through the second half of 1766 and most of 1767, the people of the colonies happily basked in their victory over the Stamp Act. But Samuel Adams and James Otis did not relax their efforts. Adams wrote on December 11, 1766, "I am still upon the Libertys of the Colonys." They kept up their constant barrage of letters to the newspapers, to the other colonies, and to London. They arranged through the Caucus Club for John Hancock to be elected to the Massachusetts House of Representatives. They succeeded in ridding the Council of men loyal to Governor Francis Bernard, who would support any acts Parliament might pass. Thomas Hutchinson and his relatives Andrew and Peter Oliver, the most important men in the colony, no longer had seats on the Council.

Samuel Adams had himself elected clerk of the House of Representatives. It was a position of much power, and it paid £100 a year, which Adams and his family needed. When James Otis was vetoed as Speaker of the House of Representatives by Governor Bernard, Adams had his old friend and political ally Thomas Cushing Junior made Speaker.

By now all the colonies were divided into two political parties. The Tories were loyal to the king and Parliament. The other party was the Whigs, who were also loyal to the king. But they strongly defended the liberties granted in the royal charters against assaults by Parliament. In Massachusetts, the Whigs were in full control of both the House of Representatives and the Council, thanks to the political maneuvers of Samuel Adams and James Otis.

But the Tory newspapers never let the townspeople forget that Adams should be in jail as a tax defaulter. He was sued in court twice. The first time he won, the second time he lost. Adams petitioned the Boston town meeting for more time to come up with the money. Eventually, he became so powerful in

Boston government that he only paid a small amount to settle his much greater debt.

In September 1767, word reached the colonies that a new set of taxes had been passed by Parliament—they were part of the Townshend Acts. Lead, glass, paint, paper, and tea—all of which the colonists had previously imported in large amounts—were going to be taxed starting in November 1767. The new Townshend taxes were to be paid as a duty, or import tax—the kind of external tax the colonies said they would accept. But the Townshend Acts directed that money collected from the taxes would go to pay the salaries of judges and others in high positions in the colonial government. The money would also provide for those 10,000 soldiers to defend the frontier forts. The colonists did not like the idea of judges, royal governors, and other government officials being paid by these taxes. The colonial legislatures had always paid their salaries; that gave them control over government officials. In addition to the taxes, the Townshend Acts established in Boston a Board of Customs Commissioners that would strictly collect duties on imported goods. Anyone caught smuggling would be tried in one of four vice-admiralty courts set up in Boston, Philadelphia, Charleston, and Halifax. These courts would try cases without juries, since probably no colonial jury would convict a smuggler. Taking away trials by jury really angered the colonists because trial by jury was a basic right of every "Englishman."

A town meeting was called. As a way to fight back, Samuel Adams strongly encouraged that a nonconsumption agreement be adopted. The people would be asked to sign a pledge not to buy a long list of articles, mostly luxury goods, imported from Great Britain. Adams thought that if British merchants could not sell their goods in Boston, they might put pressure on Parliament to repeal the Townshend Acts just as they had pressured Parliament to repeal the Stamp Act. In many of the colonies women formed groups called Daughters of Liberty to support the boycott. They insisted on making homespun cloth to replace British cloth and refused to buy tea for their households.

Early in 1768, Samuel Adams drafted a special letter protesting the new taxes. He and James Otis got the General Court to adopt what became known as the Massachusetts Circular Letter, which was sent to the legislatures of all the other colonies. The letter proposed that "all possible Care should be taken, that the Representations of the several Assembly upon so delicate a point, should harmonize with each other" on the new taxes. The letter stated that the Townshend duties were revenue-raising taxes that violated their constitutional rights.

The Massachusetts Circular Letter claimed that colonists were not represented in the British Parliament and so could not be taxed "without their consent." They had their own colonial legislatures to represent and tax themselves. Moreover, paying salaries to the governor, judges, and other officials without the "consent of the people & at their expense" undermined the principles of fairness and endangered their "happiness and security." It also notified the other colonies that Massachusetts had sent a letter to the British government protesting their having to provide and pay for supplies for British soldiers. The letter asked other colonies what further proposals they might have. After these attacks on the British Parliament, the Massachusetts Circular Letter ended with the statement that this "House cannot conclude without expressing their firm Confidence in the King our common head & Father, that the united & dutifull Supplications [humble requests] of his distressed American Subjects will meet with his royal & favorable Acceptance."

But the Adams-inspired Massachusetts Circular Letter set off a firestorm when government officials in London read it. Some members of Parliament became convinced that the colonies were united and ready to revolt. The British government sent to the colonial governors letters condemning the Massachusetts Circular Letter. It ordered them to prevent their colonial legislatures from supporting that document. But several colonial assemblies had already voted their approval.

The British government sent off a letter to Governor Francis Bernard. It demanded that the Massachusetts House of Representatives rescind, that is, cancel, the Circular Letter. If the House refused to do so, it should be dissolved. These British demands seemed so dictatorial that they kindled the wrath of the Americans again. The Massachusetts House voted 92 to 17 to defy Parliament. But those 17 who voted for rescinding were held up to ridicule and persecution. Their names were hung on the Liberty Tree and posted in the newspapers. Within months, seven of them were voted out of office for daring to disagree.

When the representatives refused to rescind the Circular Letter, Governor Bernard dismissed them until they were ready to rescind it. The representatives turned the tables on the governor, however, by voting 99 to 3 to write to the king and ask him to recall Bernard for slandering the people of Massachusetts.

The House of Representatives took this action because they had learned that the governor, the lieutenant governor, the secretary of the province, and others had been writing alarmist letters to London telling the British government how disloyal the people were in Massachusetts. These men had been doing this ever since the Stamp Act protests. It was little wonder that the Circular Letter created such an uproar in Great Britain.

The letters from royal officials in Massachusetts caused the British government to become alarmed enough to send a 50-gun ship, the *Romney*, to Boston Harbor by late spring of 1768. It anchored offshore and aimed its guns at the heart of Boston.

With the *Romney* to back them up, the customs commissioners, who had been having a hard time collecting any taxes, boldly seized John Hancock's ship *Liberty* for smuggling wine. Word quickly spread, and a mob of townspeople gathered on the wharf. To show the crowd who was in charge now, the customs commissioners signaled the *Romney* to tow the *Liberty* out into the harbor and tie it alongside under its big guns. This further enraged the crowd. They bombarded the commissioners with rocks, tore their clothes, and broke their swords. The mob followed them home and attacked their houses, breaking windows and yelling threats. When the governor complained, Adams said the people had the right to protest the illegal taking of the *Liberty*.

This was no ordinary mob. These people were trained to terrorize others into doing what they wanted them to do. Operating by night, they blackened their faces, wore nightcaps over their heads, and howled a lot. People were afraid of what they *might* do rather than what they actually *did*. Much property damage was done, but no one was killed. Three of their victims were tarred and feathered—a fate almost worse than being killed. It was enough to scare others. This was Samuel Adams's idea of liberty and rights—organized lawlessness. "The end will justify the means," he said often, or so one of his enemies claimed he said.

These scare tactics worked on the commissioners. They were so frightened, they fled Boston for safety aboard the *Romney*. There they stayed for nine days until they were transferred to Castle Island in Boston Harbor. In fear for their lives, they refused to return unless British troops were sent. The governor sent more letters to London saying he was helpless to control Boston's mob.

All during the summer of 1768 rumors that troops were to be sent to occupy Boston circulated in the town. Bostonians realized that troops over which they had no control could take away their liberties. People who had always considered Samuel Adams a troublemaker now supported him.

In August, with tensions high and the *Romney*'s guns aimed at the town, Boston merchants drew up a nonimportation agreement to add to the previous year's pledge by townspeople not to buy British goods. The merchants agreed not to import British goods until January 1770. They knew that if they did not agree, the Sons of Liberty would pay them a visit. Or children would stand outside their shops and throw mud on their customers.

The positive response of Bostonians to the goods boycott and of the merchants to the nonimportation agreement, as well as the people's fear of British troops, gave Adams the courage to call a convention of delegates sent from every town in Massachusetts. They met in Faneuil Hall on September 22. The delegates knew that there were 15,000 trained militiamen in Massachusetts, excellent marksmen, many with experience in the French and Indian War. Adams hoped these veterans could beat back any troops that tried to land in Boston. He had 4,000 muskets, with ball and powder, stacked in Faneuil Hall free to any man who wanted one. But the conservative delegates from rural Massachusetts told the riotous Bostonians they would not fight. Then New York sent word it would not join Massachusetts in armed rebellion. Adams had to back down. Even he was forced to realize the time was not yet right for war. But Adams was never without a backup plan. All right, the Sons of Liberty would not

Paul Revere's engraving of British ships landing troops in Boston in 1768.

revolt yet; they would just make things difficult for the soldiers.

Five hundred British troops of the 14th and 29th Regiments of infantry plus some artillery landed in Boston on October 1, 1768. They were greeted with angry silence by most people. Only the Tories were glad to see them. The troops, who were expecting the worst, were fully armed with 16 rounds of powder and ball. Their fixed bayonets glittered in the sunlight. Dressed in bright red uniform jackets, they paraded up King Street to a public field known as Boston Common, drums beating, high-pitched fifes playing .

Now what was to be done with 500 British soldiers? The early October weather was crisp and sunny. The coming New England winter would be long and cold. Under the Quartering Act, first passed in 1765 and renewed yearly, Parliament required that the colonial governments provide housing, food, fuel, beer or cider, and candles for the troops. The soldiers did not have to pay for any of this. The colonies had always refused to do this. After all, being required to provide those things was just like being required to pay a tax for which they had not given their consent. The Council told Lieutenant Colonel William Dalrymple, who was in charge of the troops, that as many soldiers as possible should be housed at Fort William on Castle Island. According to the Council, that was the law. Samuel Adams discussed the law in the *Boston Gazette* on October 10. "[T]he civil officers and No OTHERS are empower'd and required to quarter and billet [to assign lodging by a billet, or official order] the officers and soldiers in his Majesty's service IN THE BARRACKS PROVIDED in the Colonies, and if there shall not be sufficient room in the said Barracks for the Officers and Soldiers, THEN AND IN SUCH CASE ONLY, to quarter and billet the residue [remainder] of them in the inns, livery stables and other houses mentioned in said act."

In October 1768, two regiments of British infantry entered Boston and marched through the streets unopposed.

But Castle Island was three miles out in the harbor. The troops had been sent to keep order in Boston itself. During the first weeks, some of the troops lived in tents on Boston Common. Others were temporarily housed in Faneuil Hall. Some even camped out right in front of John Adams's house on Cole Lane near Brattle Square. He was not pleased to be awakened at all hours by those infernal fifes playing, drums beating, feet marching on cobblestones. General Thomas Gage, who was in charge of all British troops in North America, came to Boston in the middle of October. He insisted the troops remain in town.

When General Gage asked for supplies, he was told the House of Representatives had been dissolved and could not order such supplies for him. When parties of soldiers went out to find food at farms in the country, they were told it had been a bad crop year and there was nothing to spare. Gage finally rented space in vacant warehouses near the Custom House and paid for supplies rather than have a confrontation with the stubborn Americans.

At first, all was law and order. Soldiers patrolled the streets and alleys during the day and especially at night. On November 10, two more regiments arrived. The troops set up a cannon facing the Town House where the Massachusetts General Court met, and they pointed it toward the doors. They pushed people on the streets out of their way with their bayonets; they sometimes stole property; they searched people for no reason. To turn people of all the colonies against the troops, Samuel Adams wrote melodramatic articles for the newspapers. He elevated these incidents to atrocities—beatings of children, public drunkenness, violating the Sabbath, and of course, insults and worse to girls and women. He even wrote about how the soldiers had shot and wounded his faithful dog, Queue. In the *Boston Gazette* of December 5, 1768, Adams wrote the following:

> I am informed that not less than nine gentlemen of character, some of them of the first families in the province, were stop'd and put under guard the other evening. . . . And still more alarming, that one of his Majesty's Council, was stop'd in his chariot [a four-wheeled horse-drawn carriage] in the daytime, when

going out of town, under a flimsy pretense that possibly he might have conceal'd a [British] deserter in his chariot and was treated with insolence.

The people of the other colonies were willing to believe the exaggerations and half-truths in these stories. In Boston, these reports increased the people's fear and hatred.

Yet the troops had been given strict orders from Parliament itself that they were under the control of Massachusetts civilian government. They could not take any action unless asked to do so by the Council or by a justice of the peace. They were acting as a police force. If fired upon by civilians, they could not fire back.

When Boston remained more or less peaceful, the British government withdrew two of its four regiments and sent them back to Halifax, Nova Scotia. This left only 500 troops in Boston. There were suspected to be many more than 500 Sons of Liberty.

Governor Francis Bernard announced another departure—his own. He said Parliament had asked him to return to London to give a report on the situation in Boston. Rather than going home in disgrace, he had been given a title by the king. He would leave as Sir Francis Bernard of Nettleham. Bernard had made himself very unpopular with everyone including some Tories. It was his hysterical letters that brought the troops to Boston. Someone even cut the heart out of a portrait of him that hung in Harvard College. On the night he sailed, July 31, 1769, all the church bells rang and Boston threw an enormous celebration for itself. But his departure left Thomas Hutchinson as acting governor.

James Otis soon had another score to settle with Hutchinson. More letters to Bernard, Hutchinson, and the customs commissioners defaming Boston's people came to light. In one letter, Otis was accused of being a traitor. In a frenzy of anger, he went alone to the British Coffee House where he confronted Custom Commissioner John Robinson. He particularly blamed Robinson for this terrible accusation. Otis called Robinson vile names, and Robinson struck Otis on the head with his sword, making a deep wound. A brawl followed in which Otis was badly beaten. Although a brilliant man, Otis had been the victim of mental illness off and on for years. His injuries drove him over the brink into insanity. He had to be taken to the country to live out his life. This left Samuel Adams in charge of Boston.

The brutal attack on Otis angered the townspeople. They had looked up to Otis as a leader for years. This attack was the most notorious one of thousands of scuffles that occurred between townspeople and soldiers day and night. Knowing that the soldiers could not fire on them, men, boys, and even women took to harassing them, calling them "bloody backs" and "Tommy Lobsters," because of their red coats. The soldiers had their revenge in dark alleys and tavern brawls.

With the coming of 1770, the Boston merchants' nonimportation agreement ran out. Adams had spread the nonimportation agreement to New York and Philadelphia after he appealed to the local chapters of the Sons of Liberty in those colonies to pressure the merchants to agree. But some Boston merchants thought they had lost enough money and refused to be terrorized by the Sons of Liberty into complying any more.

On the night of February 22, 1770, a mob gathered before the house of a merchant and Tory informer named Ebenezer Richardson. When they broke his windows, Richardson fired his musket at them. He didn't fire bullets, but swan shot, similar to beebees. Unfortunately, several of the shots hit Christopher Snider, an 11-year-old boy in the crowd. It was enough to kill him.

The Sons of Liberty seized Richardson and brought him before a justice of the peace who put him in the gaol, or jail, for his own safety. Samuel Adams saw to it that the child had the largest funeral ever held in the colonies. The procession formed under the Liberty Tree. Weeping thousands lined the route as the small coffin and the mourners passed on the way to a grave on the Common. Christopher was given the title of littlest martyr.

A week after Christopher Snider was killed, a big fight broke out between off-duty soldiers and shipyard workers on Friday, March 2. A soldier, looking for work, had gone to Grey's Ropewalk, where rope used on ships was made from hemp. He was offered the job of cleaning an outhouse. This insult could not go unanswered. He went back to his barracks and returned with some friends, spoiling for a fight. They got one. But the soldiers ended up getting the worst of it. The next two days, laborers taunted and threw snowballs at the soldiers. The soldiers, on duty and tightly disciplined by their officers, did not reply.

John Adams believed these encounters were not accidental meetings. The laborers and foot soldiers were being used to create some sort of *incident.* He believed this was the wrong way to get rid of the soldiers.

On the evening of Monday, March 5, a lone soldier named Hugh Montgomery stood guard duty in front of the Custom House on King Street. He was being pelted with snowballs by boys. Then a crowd of several hundred men and boys gathered and threw pieces of ice, sharp seashells, and the worst of names. It was strange that they were out in the streets because over a foot of snow had fallen. This was a night to stay by the hearth. Backed by the crowd, a young apprentice boldly stepped up and called the lone sentry names, daring him to fire. Montgomery hit him a light blow with the butt of his musket, and the boy fell down. The crowd of men pushed toward the soldier accusing him of attempted murder. They cried, "Kill him! Kill him!"

Suddenly a church bell began ringing, the warning signal that a fire had broken out. This immediately brought people out of their houses into the streets looking for the fire to fight. There was no fire, but there was mass confusion.

Montgomery loaded his musket and pointed it at the crowd, which had grown even larger. The crowd yelled, "The lobster dare not fire!" Montgomery called to the guardhouse across the street for the main guard to turn out. Instantly, eight soldiers and an officer, Captain Thomas Preston, pushed their way through the crowd with bayonets, coming to the aid of Montgomery. The captain ordered his men to load their muskets. Several men in the crowd sensed the great danger. They pleaded with people to go home. Preston stood in front of his men so they could not fire and joined in the pleadings.

Instead, the crowd rushed the soldiers. Someone hit Preston a hard blow on his arm and pushed him out of the way. Montgomery was knocked down. The pushing and shoving continued until someone yelled "Fire!"

Seven of the eight soldiers fired their guns. When the smoke cleared, four men lay dead in the snow, a fifth was wounded.

Shocked and frightened, the crowd fell back, tripping over one another. Soldiers poured into the streets with bayonets fixed.

Lieutenant Governor Hutchinson was summoned. He fought his way through the crowds to the Town House near the scene of the shootings. From the balcony, he told the people to go to their homes. He promised justice would be done. Confused and afraid of more killings, they quietly obeyed him. Officers ordered their men to return to their barracks.

Candles burned in the Council Chamber of the Town House until three o'clock in the morning. The governor and Council members questioned witnesses and tried to decide what to do. By dawn, they had issued arrest warrants for Captain Preston and the eight soldiers. The charge—murder. They prayed this would prevent an uprising by the people and more blood in the snow.

Paul Revere's propaganda engraving "The Bloody Massacre" showed soldiers firing upon supposedly peaceful Bostonians.

CHAPTER SIX

Master of the Puppets

BOSTON MASSACRE. That black headline topped the special March 6, 1770, edition of the *Boston Gazette*. It was accompanied by a version of the incident thought to be written by Samuel Adams, saying many citizens had been killed or wounded. The papers were snatched up by men in the streets; almost all were armed with muskets or pistols. They were frightened, angry, and confused to the point where the town was on the verge of the revolt Adams had dreamed of. In the newspaper was the announcement of a special town meeting, or Body meeting as it was now called, to be held at eleven o'clock at Faneuil Hall. Samuel Adams had long packed town meetings with the meaner sort who were not legally entitled to vote. Those who could vote stayed away, for they feared they might be attacked or their property destroyed. This day virtually every male citizen of Boston tried to crowd into Faneuil Hall. Here Samuel Adams made an impassioned speech. But it was not an appeal for calm and cool-headedness in his near hysterical listeners. He harangued the meeting, shouting that removal of the troops was the only way to prevent more bloodshed.

The meeting appointed a committee of 15 to call on the lieutenant governor and the Council. With Adams and Hancock in the lead, the committee and much of the meeting marched to the Town House, which overlooked the site of the massacre.

In the Council Chamber, Lieutenant Governor Hutchinson, Lieutenant Colonel Dalrymple, and the 28 weary Council members received them. Adams told them that the citizens demanded the immediate removal of all the British soldiers from the town. Hutchinson calmly replied he had no authority over the king's soldiers. Adams countered by quoting the Massachusetts charter, which said the governor was commander-in-chief of all soldiers and sailors in the colony.

After conferring with Lieutenant Colonel Dalrymple, Hutchinson offered to remove the 29th Regiment, which had been involved in the shooting, to Fort William on Castle Island. The remaining 14th Regiment would be confined to barracks.

Adams said, "If you have the power to remove *one* regiment, you have the power to remove *both*. . . . It is at your peril if you refuse. The meeting is composed of three thousand people. They

After the Boston Massacre, Adams met with Hutchinson and demanded the removal of British troops from Boston.

are become impatient. A thousand men are already arrived from the neighborhood, and the whole country is in motion. Night is approaching. An immediate answer is expected. Both regiments or none!" Hutchinson and Dalrymple knew Adams's threat was not empty. Their spies in the country towns reported Sons of Liberty all over Massachusetts were ready and waiting to march to the rescue of Boston. Hutchinson and Dalrymple gave in. The troops were all removed in a week. But feeling was so strong in the town, a Son of Liberty had to march beside the troops as they went to the wharf so the townspeople would not attack them. It was a great victory for Samuel Adams. From then on, the 14th and 29th were nicknamed the Sam Adams regiments.

The funeral of the four slaughtered martyrs, as Samuel Adams called them, was scheduled for noon on Thursday, March 8. The two previous days, Crispus Attucks and James Caldwell had lain in state at Faneuil Hall. Crispus Attucks, of African and Natick (Native American) heritage, had been the first killed in the Boston Massacre. James Caldwell was a ship's mate. Thousands of Boston citizens passed by and paid their respects—and also refueled their anger. The bodies of the ropemaker Samuel Gray and the 17-year-old apprentice Samuel Maverick were laid out at home. Patrick Carr was still alive.

As the church bells tolled, the hearses carrying the bodies passed the Custom House on King Street where the killings had occurred. Thousands of people from Boston and surrounding towns marched in the funeral procession to Granary Burying Ground where the four martyrs were laid to rest together.

Next, Samuel Adams turned to the goal of a speedy trial and hanging for Captain Preston and the soldiers. But the day after the shootings, a wealthy merchant named James Forrester with the strange nickname the "Irish Infant" burst into the law office of John Adams. Forrester begged Adams to defend Preston. He had asked all the Tory lawyers in town. They had refused, fearing what the Sons of Liberty would do to them. Forrester had persuaded young Josiah Quincy, a Whig, to agree to defend Preston, but only if John Adams would serve as the senior lawyer. John Adams was a Son of Liberty himself. But he was also a man with a strong conscience who had to do what was right or he could not live with himself. John Adams thought everyone accused of a crime should be entitled to a lawyer, no matter what he might have done. When word got out that John Adams was going to defend the hated soldiers, his law practice dropped to nothing. He was spat upon and called names in the street. He feared the Sons of Liberty would turn against him and kill him. But he did not resign as Preston's lawyer. To see justice done was a point of honor with him.

Surprisingly, Samuel Adams approved of what his cousin had undertaken. It was not a matter of family loyalty. Samuel Adams wanted the soldiers to have the best defense possible so that no one could say they were unfairly treated or that their rights were not protected. He just did not think any jury could possibly find them innocent. He wanted the trial to take place immediately while the people were still angry.

But Lieutenant Governor Hutchinson forced the trial to be postponed until the fall. John Adams was pleased; Samuel Adams was furious. There was talk of a lynching from the Liberty Tree. Extra guards were posted around the jail.

Meanwhile, on March 12, a town meeting appointed a committee to write a report to be sent to England to explain how the innocent, peaceful Bostonians were fired upon by the soldiers. Samuel Adams, of course, headed the committee. The report was titled "A short Narrative of the horrid Massacre in Boston, perpetuated in the Evening of the Fifth Day of March, 1770 by Soldiers of the XXIXth Regiment, which with the XIVth Regiment, was then quartered there, with some observations on the State of Things prior to that Catastrophy." Adams's version of the Boston Massacre took up 34 pages. In the remaining 132 pages were 96 statements from eyewitnesses.

Lieutenant Governor Hutchinson had already secretly sent Customs Commissioner Robinson to the king with his account of the shooting. Adams hired a fast ship and sent his report to powerful friends in England so Boston would not be punished. On the cover of the report was an engraving by Paul Revere showing the soldiers shooting the people. The engraving was completely false in its representation of what actually happened. But it was very important in shaping public opinion. Adams's report was not circulated in Boston, however, until after the trials were over.

Captain Thomas Preston's trial was first. It started on October 24, 1770. By this time, John Adams was convinced Preston and the soldiers were innocent. First, he made sure none of the jurors were Sons of Liberty. In fact, five jurors were Tories. Preston denied he ever gave the order to the soldiers to fire their guns. Witnesses said that people in the crowd yelled "fire" in the confusion. The most important testimony of all came from Patrick Carr, who had been mortally wounded the night of March 5, but did not die until March 14. Dr. John Jeffries, who had taken care of him, said Carr was from Ireland where British troops had cruelly persecuted the Irish for centuries. Carr had no reason to protect the British troops in Boston. Yet the doctor and witnesses heard him say the soldiers were much threatened and abused by the crowd. Their lives were in danger, and they had fired in self-defense. Carr even forgave them for killing him. Others testified that Preston's arm had almost been broken by a blow from a heavy piece of wood and that he was bruised all over. The captain was acquitted on October 30.

The eight soldiers were put on trial on November 27. John Adams defended them as he had Thomas Preston. It was known that only seven shots had been fired. Since each musket could fire only once before reloading, one gun had not been fired. It could not be determined which man had not fired. It was also known that Montgomery and a man named Kilroi had fired their guns. Kilroi had even bayoneted Sam Gray's dead body. Montgomery and Kilroi were found guilty. By a twist of the law, they pleaded "benefit of clergy" and recited the 51st Psalm to show they could read. This procedure was sometimes used to lessen the harshness of criminal laws. In this case, it kept them from being executed. The charge against them was reduced to manslaughter, the unlawful but unintentional killing of others. Instead of execution, the two men's punishment was to be branded on the left thumb in open court with a red-hot branding iron. Despite more than 100 written testimonies and two trials, no one has ever been able to learn with certainty exactly what happened the night of March 5, 1770, on King Street in Boston over 200 years ago. Ironically, word arrived in Boston months later that on

Samuel Adams influenced many Puritan ministers to preach against the colonial tax policies of the British Parliament.

March 5, Parliament had begun to debate the repeal of the Townshend Acts.

Samuel Adams, of course, was furious with the outcome of the trial. He discounted Patrick Carr's testimony by saying Carr was a Catholic and could not be believed anyway. After the trial was over, he wrote a series of 10 articles about it. He did not try to rouse the people. But through his own logic, putting in some information and ignoring other facts, he analyzed and rationalized until it was hard not to be convinced he was right. Samuel Adams was a master of the art of argument. He did not let people forget the Boston Massacre either. Every March 5 for years afterward, he staged a grand memorial.

Nevertheless, Samuel Adams did not hold the acquittals against his cousin John. He saw to it that John Adams was elected to the House of Representatives. There was much grumbling in Boston about the verdict. From their pulpits, the "Black Regiment" preached against what they regarded as a miscarriage of justice. But people were glad it was over, and many regretted what had happened.

In order to fight for their liberties, most people had made great personal sacrifices. Because of the nonimportation agreements, few ships sailed back and forth across the Atlantic Ocean carrying cargoes between Great Britain and the North American colonies. Merchants like John Hancock had lost much business, costing thousands of pounds. Some men had gone bankrupt. Sailors, shipyard workers, clerks in stores and countinghouses, tavern owners and their employees, even churches were hurt financially. It had caused a serious business slowdown. Samuel Adams may have enjoyed poverty. Nobody else did.

By April 1770, Parliament had been forced to repeal all the Townshend taxes except the tax on tea. It also allowed the hated Quartering Act to expire. Despite these victories, Adams had tried to keep the nonimportation agreements in force, but people began to blame him for the hard times. The other major ports—New York, Philadelphia, Charleston, Baltimore—abandoned the nonimportation agreements. Prosperity returned to them. Farm products, lumber, and other exports commanded high prices. Adams continued to use terror tactics on Boston until he alienated the less radical Whigs. In 1771, even his cousin John Adams wanted nothing more to do with politics and, in disgust, moved back to his hometown of Braintree, a few miles from Boston. Most people refused to follow Samuel Adams's lead anymore. For the time being, he lost much of his political power.

Then, in 1771, Thomas Hutchinson gained new power. He was appointed the royal governor. Leaders of the British government probably thought they were doing the Province of Massachusetts Bay a favor by appointing a native son as governor. But many colonists considered Hutchinson a traitor because he did not support the charter. They also saw him as a power grabber, especially after his brother-in-law Andrew Oliver was appointed lieutenant governor. Most of the important jobs in the colony were still in the Hutchinson family.

After the repeal of the Townshend taxes, except the one on tea, members of Parliament seemed to forget about the colonies. They did not pass any more taxes on the colonies to support the North American army. Instead, they turned their attention to other parts of the far-flung British Empire.

All the colonies had agents in London to inform them about what was going on and to use their influence on behalf of the colonies' welfare. Benjamin Franklin, the agent of Pennsylvania, had helped get the Stamp Act repealed. When Massachusetts agent Dennys Debrets died, Benjamin Franklin was proposed to act as agent for Massachusetts as well as Pennsylvania. After all, he had been born and raised in Boston. A man of much natural charm, he was well liked by almost everyone except Samuel Adams, though the two men had never met. Franklin was a Quaker, a religious group that the Puritans had persecuted earlier in Massachusetts's history. Furthermore, Adams could not trust a man who held an appointment from the king as deputy postmaster of the colonies. Also, Franklin had a son with a woman to whom he was not married and that son was the royal governor of the colony of New Jersey. But the House of Representatives liked Franklin and voted two to one to hire him, over Adams's objections, as the agent for the Province of Massachusetts Bay.

Perhaps to prove his worth and loyalty to the Massachusetts colony, Franklin obtained 13 very private letters written in the late 1760s. Six were written by Thomas Hutchinson, four by Andrew Oliver, and two by other Tories. The letters had been sent to personal friends in England. Franklin sent the letters to Thomas Cushing, the Speaker of the Massachusetts House of Representatives, with the warning that they must be kept secret, must not be published, and must be returned to him in England.

Samuel Adams and others hinted darkly that a great scandal had been discovered. Before the letters were read, the House of Representatives was cleared of visitors and the doors were locked. This only added to the mystery and heightened the drama. The letters proved beyond a doubt who had put the colony through the ordeal of soldiers, customs commissioners, and taxes.

Most of what was in the letters Hutchinson had said in public many times. But Adams and a committee constructed a pamphlet that printed out-of-context statements from the letters. Hutchinson had spoken against the town meetings but only because they had come to be misused. He had urged that judges and other officials be paid by the government in London rather than by the colonial government. This suggestion became part of the hated Townshend Acts. Worst of all was Hutchinson's statement that the colonies could not and should not enjoy the same liberties as Englishmen in Great Britain. "[T]here must be an abridgment [reduction] of what are called English liberties. . . . I doubt whether it is possible to project a system of government in which a colony three thousand miles distant from the parent state shall enjoy all the liberty of the parent state." As for the other letters Franklin had obtained, those written by Oliver and others had proposed changes in the charter and a Council appointed by the king.

Copies of the letters themselves and Adams's pamphlet with his edited version of the letters were sent to all the colonies. They so angered people that Hutchinson's effigy was burned in Philadelphia, Pennsylvania, and Princeton, New Jersey.

On June 23, 1773, the Massachusetts General Court sent a petition to the king to recall Hutchinson as governor of the colony. The House of Representatives voted 80 to 11 in favor of the petition. "[T]he said Thos Hutchinson Esqr and Andrew

Oliver Esqr have by their above mentioned Conduct and otherwise rendered themselves justly obnoxious to your Majestys loving Subjects, we pray that your Majesty will be graciously pleasd to remove them from their posts in this Government."

Hutchinson accused Adams of using witchcraft to make the representatives vote against their better judgment. He called Samuel Adams the "Master of the puppets." The king's advisers, of course, turned down the colonists' request and used a lot of impressive words to call the petitioners troublemakers. Hutchinson continued in his post of royal governor, but for the most part in name only. Samuel Adams really ruled Boston.

Benjamin Franklin paid for his efforts as agent for the Massachusetts colony and his betrayal by Samuel Adams. When the British government learned he had sent private letters to Massachusetts, he was called before the king's ministers, or advisers, and denounced. For an hour, the 68-year-old man was forced to stand and listen to his accusers attack his behavior in the worst of terms. Not only was Franklin called a man without honor and a thief, he lost his job as deputy postmaster for the North American colonies. After that, the "better sort" of English society refused to associate with him. The whole affair was very damaging to his excellent reputation and his usefulness as an agent.

Although the plot against Hutchinson and his family using their private letters was successful, many of Samuel Adams's efforts to fuel people's anger against Great Britain and its colonial representatives fizzled. From the end of the Boston Massacre trials in late 1770 until the middle of 1772, there had been a lull in tensions between Great Britain and its colonies. Economic conditions greatly improved. Almost nobody paid attention to Adams's gloom and doom writings. Yet he refused to remain idle. By the fall of 1772, Samuel Adams was busy developing a new way of organizing successful protests—committees of correspondence. He urged that committees of correspondence be formed in the towns of Massachusetts and the other colonies. The purpose of the committees was to keep each other informed about the acts of the British government.

Samuel Adams persuaded the Boston town meeting to

Benjamin Franklin was called before the Lords of the Privy Council and criticized for publicizing Hutchinson's letters.

appoint a 21-member committee of correspondence. Samuel Adams described it this way: "[W]e are a Committee, not of the Trade, but of the whole Town; chosen to be as it were outguards to watch the Designs [plans] of our Enemies . . . & to establish an Union which is formidable to our Adversaries." At first, members of the committees of correspondence usually were the leading Whig radicals like Samuel Adams. These men came to know each other very well by letter if not in person. Over the next few years, more artisans and farmers joined.

When the proposal for the formation of the Boston Committee of Correspondence was to be voted on by the House of Representatives, Governor Hutchinson tried to dissolve the House before it could vote. He saw the forming of such a committee as a step toward union of the colonies—a thing greatly feared by the Tories. But Samuel Adams as clerk of the House locked the door to keep the governor out until the vote was taken. Naturally his proposal won the vote.

The British government had reason to worry about the committees of correspondence that towns were setting up in 1772 and 1773. In November 1772, Samuel Adams had presented to the Boston town meeting a declaration called the *State of the Rights of the Colonists*. He had written it as a member of the

Boston Committee of Correspondence. After the town meeting approved it, the radical document was sent to other towns.

In the *State of the Rights of the Colonists*, Adams bluntly declared that "[a]mong the natural rights of the colonist are these: first, a right to life; second, to liberty; third, to property; together with the right to support and defend them in the best manner they can." The phrase "to defend them in the best manner they can" could be and probably was read as a threat to British authority.

Adams listed the various rights the colonists had "as Men, as Christians, and as Subjects." He directly attacked the new British policy that prevented colonial legislatures from voting on and paying the royal governors' and the judges' salaries. Judges should be "impartial judges in all cases that may happen." He claimed that "governors have no right to seek what they please." Furthermore, in answer to British attempts to tax the colonies, he wrote that the government could not "justly take from any man any part of his property, without his consent, in person or by his representative."

State of the Rights of the Colonies ended as bluntly as it began. Adams asked the colonists to consider how long they would—or should—continue to accept such bad treatment from Great Britain. "The colonists have been branded with the odious [hateful] names of traitors and rebels only for complaining of their grievances; How long such treatment will or ought to be borne [put up with] is submitted."

CHAPTER SEVEN

The World's Biggest Tea Party

When the Townshend Acts were repealed, taxes were taken off lead, glass, paint, and paper. But the tax on tea stayed, more as a symbol that Parliament had the right to tax the colonies than as a money source. Adams, who saw a threat to liberty behind every tree, damned the tea tax. He called anyone who bought English tea a traitor. It was not as much of an issue as Adams tried to make it seem. Most tea used in the colonies was smuggled in from the Netherlands anyway because it was cheaper.

Early in 1773, the East India Company in England faced bankruptcy. Many English people owned stock in the company. It also paid the British treasury £400,000 every year for the privilege of doing business in India. If the East India Company went broke, it would ruin Great Britain's economy. It certainly would bring down the British government.

The East India Company had 17 million pounds of tea stored in its London warehouses. If it could be sold, the company and the British economy would be saved. The East India Company asked the British government to give it the monopoly on the tea trade with the American colonies duty free, meaning it would pay no taxes when it sold the tea. The British government agreed to the tea monopoly but said the import tax on tea must remain. However, the British government would charge only half what people in Great Britain paid, a tax of a mere three pence per pound when the low-priced tea was brought into the colonies. The East India Company and the British government were certain the colonies would buy the tea because it would be cheaper and better than the tea smuggled in from the Netherlands. Everybody supposedly would be a winner—the British government, the East India Company, and the colonies. Smuggling would be stopped. Of course, only the East India Company could ship and sell the tea and only to certain merchants in the colonies whom they chose—people like Governor Thomas Hutchinson's sons. Previously, the company had sold its tea at auctions in England, and anyone could buy it. This new monopoly made the other American merchants angry because most of them would not be allowed to sell the tea. Also the cheap but better tea would compete against their illegal Dutch tea and end their profitable smuggling. The Tea Act was passed by Parliament on May 10, 1773.

No one thought it would cause a protest. But the East India Company and the British government did not realize that the boycott of English tea, ongoing since 1767, would not end no matter how cheap the tea was. The import duty of three pence per pound was still taxation without representation. Samuel Adams called the duty on the tea a tribute that would be followed by taxes on everything exported by Great Britain. At last, Samuel Adams had a new cause to rouse the people—and the new committees of correspondence were ready to leap into action.

After the Tea Act of 1773 went into effect, Adams wasted no time and wrote to the other colonies about it: "We cannot close without mentioning a fresh Instance of the temper & Design of the British Ministry; and that is in allowing the East India Company, with a View of pacifying them, to ship their Tea to America. . . . How necessary then is it that Each Colony should take effectual methods to prevent this measure from having its designed Effects."

The Sons of Liberty went to work again. In Charleston, the tea was landed, but it was left to rot. In Philadelphia, the merchants whom the East India Company had designated to sell their tea were forced to resign. That was because Philadelphia had passed a resolve that all who sold the East India tea were to be treated as public enemies. When the tea ships headed toward Philadelphia, they were denied entrance to the Delaware River and sent back to England. The same was done in New York. New Jersey refused to let the tea be put ashore.

In Boston, the Hutchinsons and a merchant family named Clarke, who were to sell the tea, were ordered to appear at the Liberty Tree at noon on November 3, 1773. The bells were rung in all the churches, and a crowd of 1,000 gathered. But the would-be

East India tea merchants did not appear. They had barricaded themselves in Clarke's warehouse. A committee was sent forth from the Liberty Tree to tell them to send the tea ships back when they arrived. From inside the warehouse, the Clarkes and Hutchinsons shouted no. They would store the tea when it landed and await further orders from London. The Sons of Liberty shouted threats of what would happen to them if they did not agree. A few days later, a mob broke windows in Clarke's house, and the tea merchants fled to Castle Island.

On Sunday, November 28, the first of the tea ships, the *Dartmouth*, arrived in Boston and tied up at Griffen's Wharf. Immediately, Sons of Liberty took up guard posts to make sure no tea was put ashore. A few days later, two more ships, the *Beaver* and the *Eleanor*, arrived. Between the three ships, they carried 342 chests of tea valued at £19,000 (about $85,000).

The Tea Act and sea laws were very complicated. The Sons of Liberty could not let the tea be put ashore and the duty, or taxes, paid because that would spoil the united boycott of the colonies. But if it was not landed in 20 days after arriving, the governor could call the troops from Castle Island and land it by force. Governor Hutchinson said he could not let the ships leave Boston unless the duty was paid or he would be breaking a 72-year-old colonial law. Even if the ships were sent back to England with the tea, they would be seized by the British government and the ships' owner would be ruined financially. Why the ships were not stopped outside the harbor and sent back to England as happened in New York and Philadelphia is not known. They would not have been subject to seizure if that had been done.

Once the ships were in port, there was a terrible confusion of laws. But Adams solved the problem boldly. He called a town meeting for December 16. The owner of the *Dartmouth* was sent twice to ask Hutchinson to let the ships sail back to England without paying the tax. It was night by the time the second refusal was announced to the town meeting. Then Adams said, "This meeting can do nothing more to save the country!"

Those words were a signal. From out on the street, Indian war whoops split the night. Forty to 50 men wrapped in blankets, their faces darkened, and carrying axes charged toward Griffen's

Wharf and the tea ships. The townspeople followed. Thousands stood silently on the shore for three hours watching the men disguised as "Indians" attack the tea ships in the bright moonlight.

Conveniently, the captains of the ships were not on board; the crews stood aside and made no attempt to interfere. The tea chests, which weighed 450 pounds each, were hauled up from the holds onto the decks. With their tomahawks, the "Indians" smashed the chests and dumped the loose tea leaves over the side into Boston Harbor. Except for the sharp cracking noise of the axes and the splash of the tea, there was no sound—no cursing, no protesting crew, no triumphant "Indians." When the last of the chests had been thrown overboard, tea that had spilled on the decks was swept up and thrown overboard, too. Then the "Indians" left. No one was killed or injured. No property was damaged—except the tea. All this was done while British warships rode at anchor less than half a mile away.

The work of dumping the tea was done by strong young men brought in from the country so no one would recognize them. However, Boston Sons of Liberty officers must have been there to keep control. Although thousands watched, nobody would identify a single person who took part. No arrests were made.

The Boston Tea Party was the major turning point between Great Britain and its colonies in North America. When the news of what had happened reached London, leaders of the British government exploded in anger. They had ignored the colonists' tweaking the parent country's nose for a long time. But this was an insult that could not be patiently overlooked. Laws had been deliberately broken; valuable private property destroyed. Boston would be punished severely. The king was so angry he immediately appointed General Thomas Gage in New York to go to Boston as military governor. Parliament passed the Boston Port Bill. Lord Frederick North, the prime minister, was "[d]etermined to see America at the king's feet."

On May 10, 1774, the ship *Lively* reached Boston with news of the first punishment for the Tea Party. The Boston Port Bill stated that Boston Harbor would be closed at noon on June 1 to all incoming ships and on June 14 to all outgoing ships until the tea was paid for.

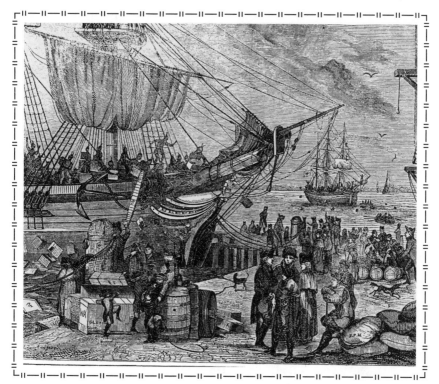

Samuel Adams planned the Boston Tea Party of 1773 during
which tea was illegally dumped into Boston Harbor.

That was not all. Colonists soon learned of other laws directed against Boston and Massachusetts. Under certain conditions,
government officials in Massachusetts accused of serious crimes
committed while they were enforcing tax laws or putting down
riots could be sent to England for their trials. These pro-British
people could therefore escape trial by jury in the Massachusetts
colony. Another law took away important parts of the
Massachusetts charter. The Council members would, in the
future, be 36 in number, and all would be appointed by the king.
Judges would be appointed by the governor and could be
removed by him. Juries would be selected by the sheriff, and
almost all town meetings were outlawed.

General Gage arrived in Boston three days after the *Lively*.
He brought troops with him—infantry, artillery, marines—some

5,000 in all. That was one soldier for every three people in Boston including children.

Samuel Adams wrote letters drumming up sympathy for the besieged city of Boston:

> The people receive this cruel edict with abhorrence and indignation. They consider themselves as suffering the stroke ministerial—I may more precisely say, Hutchinsonian vengeance. In the common cause of America. . . . Did not the very being of every sea-port town, and indeed of every Colony, considered as a free people, depend upon it, I would not even then entertain a thought so dishonorable of them as that they would leave us now to struggle alone.

On June 1 when the port of Boston closed, church bells tolled and people started wearing black clothing as if in mourning. But the day was not all bad. Samuel Adams tasted total victory in his 30-year war with Thomas Hutchinson. Hutchinson sailed for England to report to the king, and he never returned.

Four days after Hutchinson left, the Boston Committee of Correspondence presented a document called the Solemn League & Covenant that people could sign, promising that they would not do business with England and would stop using British imports after August 31. People who refused to sign were boycotted and had their names published.

At a stormy June 17 illegal town meeting, Tories came demanding that the tea be paid for so the harbor could open again. More than a few Whigs agreed with them. Benjamin Franklin had sent letter after letter from England urging the tea be paid for and all would be forgiven. He even offered to pay for it out of his own pocket. Merchants in the other colonies urged the same. But Samuel Adams convinced the people that paying for the tea would be admitting they were guilty of throwing it in the harbor. After all, some marauding "Indians" had done it, hadn't they? No one knew who any of them were, so why was Boston being punished? Radicals, like Samuel Adams, who had so carefully staged the Tea Party, wanted to make Boston a martyred city.

When General Gage came to Boston, he carried orders to arrest Samuel Adams anytime he saw fit. But Gage feared that arresting Adams would set off a violent riot. He did not want his soldiers having to kill civilians. Instead, he tried to buy Adams off. He sent a commander of one of the British regiments to warn

This 1774 British cartoon shows colonists tarring and feathering a tax collector. The Boston Tea Party is in the background.

Adams not to displease the king any further. He could be arrested and sent to England for trial and a horrible execution. However, if he would cease his activities, he would be well rewarded, "and would thereby make his peace with the King." Samuel Adams replied, "Sir, I trust I have long since made my peace with the King of kings. No personal considerations shall induce me to abandon the righteous cause of my country. Tell Governor Gage it is the advice of Samuel Adams to him no longer to insult the feelings of an exasperated people."

The other colonies were outraged at the treatment of Boston. Adams in his tidal wave of letters reminded them that it could happen to them, too. They sent supplies and money. Carolina sent rice. Cornmeal and flour came from several Massachusetts towns. Philadelphia sent money, Maryland bread. Sheep and cows were sent to be slaughtered. Even friends of America in England sent money. Adams wrote thank-you letters to everyone. To Farmington, Connecticut, which had sent 400 bushels of rye and Indian corn, he wrote, "The Committee have a very grateful sense of the generosity of their friends in Farmington. . . . The Town of Boston is now suffering for the common liberties of America, and while they are aided and supported by their friends, I am persuaded they will struggle through the conflict, firm and steady." Soon John Hancock's three-story warehouse was bulging. Adams appointed himself head of a committee to distribute the food fairly, for many people were out of work. Even Adams was not being paid his salary as clerk anymore.

Great Britain could have done nothing more to draw the colonies together than passing the hated laws punishing Boston that came to be known as the Coercive Acts or the Intolerable Acts. The other 12 colonies would not let Boston be starved into submission.

CHAPTER EIGHT

A Signer of the Declaration of Independence

All the colonies felt threatened by what had happened to Boston. It could happen to them. In fact, a fourth Coercive Act, a new Quartering Act, passed by Parliament in June 1774, did apply to all the colonies. In May and June 1774, committees of correspondence and several colonial assemblies called for a meeting of delegates from the various colonies to discuss the serious problems. Delegates from the 13 colonies were to meet together in Philadelphia on September 1, 1774, as a Continental Congress. They would consider action against the terrible new laws.

The Massachusetts House of Representatives was now meeting in Salem. On Friday, June 17, 1774, with 126 members present, Samuel Adams suddenly locked the door and put the key in his pocket. He read a resolve naming himself, John Adams, James Bowdoin, Thomas Cushing, and Robert Treat Paine to be delegates to the First Continental Congress. Taken by surprise, the House of Representatives was thrown into an uproar. Angered by Adams's high-handed methods, Tories and even some Whigs tried to defeat the measure. But Samuel Adams, the master intriguer, had made sure he had enough votes lined up to win before he ever locked the door. Only after he had everything he wanted legally approved did he unlock the door.

Although Samuel Adams was the undisputed leader (some said dictator) of Boston, he was suddenly an embarrassment. Bostonians understood his intentional poverty. But he could not be allowed to go to Philadelphia looking like a ragpicker. The most elegant men of the colonies would be there. What would they think of Massachusetts? There are several stories as to how the feat of providing proper clothes was accomplished by his friends and which ones paid for them. But by the time Samuel Adams and the other delegates left Boston on August 10, he had a trunk with two new suits, six pairs of stockings, six shirts, six pairs of new shoes with silver buckles, a new hat, gold knee buckles, and even new underwear. The anonymous donors were careful that none of the clothing was made from materials imported from England—otherwise Adams would have insisted on wearing his old clothes. Nor did Adams know whom to thank for the gold and silver coins amounting to £350 that had been given to him.

The Adams cousins and the other delegates set off in style in a carriage drawn by four horses. Two armed servants rode before the carriage, four footmen in servants' uniforms rode behind. At the age of 53, Samuel Adams went beyond the borders of the Massachusetts colony for the first time in his life. He found the Massachusetts men had become famous for their courageous stand. As they passed through towns in other colonies, they were greeted by the firing of cannons in salute, the ringing of church bells in welcome, and the offering of lavish dinners and receptions. It was little wonder that the journey took three weeks. All this high living was quite a source of wonder, even discomfort, to the Puritans so accustomed to plain and simple living.

Forty-four of the expected 56 delegates to the First Continental Congress met in Philadelphia at Carpenter's Hall on September 5. Twelve colonies—all but Georgia whose royal governor had prevented the choosing of delegates—were represented by two to five men each. These gentlemen were very different in their thinking. Some were radicals like Samuel Adams of Massachusetts and Patrick Henry of Virginia. Others were conservatives like George Washington of Virginia and John Dickinson of Pennsylvania. Most were moderates. The colonies had always been jealous and suspicious of one another. Until the Stamp Act of 1765, they had had little to do with each other. They did not even trade with each other very much. Even in the present crisis affecting them all, they could not suddenly put their past histories behind them.

While the Massachusetts delegates were hailed as heroes of the resistance, they were also viewed with suspicion. The southern delegates feared that the Bostonians wanted to take over the country. They were alarmed by Samuel Adams's use of mobs. Others, including John Adams, had misgivings about a leveling of society, getting rid of the power of the wealthy. They thought too much democracy was not a good thing. The Quakers of Pennsylvania had concerns about the New Englanders. They demanded that the Massachusetts delegates appear before them to be questioned. What about the oppression of Quakers and Baptists in Massachusetts? What about laws that compelled men to pay for building churches and supporting ministers? The Quakers wanted assurance that those laws would be repealed. Samuel Adams, in turn, suspected that the Quakers, who opposed war and therefore independence, were using this as an excuse to break up the Congress. He did not like Quakers, and he disapproved of Philadelphia with its entertainments—balls, theaters, and horse races.

Most of the delegates were deeply religious men although from different churches. They wanted to start the Congress with prayers for guidance but did not want to offend anyone. On the second day of the Congress, Samuel Adams proposed that the Reverend Mr. Jacob Duché, a Church of England minister from Philadelphia, read prayers every morning. The proposal was passed and Mr. Duché was named permanent chaplain. This one act of Samuel Adams went a long way to cement relations between the colonies.

The New England delegates tried not to attract much attention. They took little part in debates at official meetings. Adams did not talk about his dream of independence openly. He soon learned most delegates were interested only in working for the return to the freedom they had enjoyed before 1763. But they did not want, indeed they feared, independence as one of the greatest evils that could befall the colonies. Trade would be ruined; the colonies would begin fighting each other; France or Spain would conquer them. Except for periods of time in ancient Greece and Rome, most of the world had known only monarchies. What other kind of government was there? How would it work?

To even be a delegate to the Continental Congress could have been a hanging offense. Therefore, the official meetings were held behind locked doors with the delegates sworn to keep their discussions a secret. No minutes were taken. Most business was conducted in taverns or private lodgings. This was the way Samuel Adams worked best—behind the scenes. At first, he did not like the reserved George Washington. But when Adams realized that Washington, not Patrick Henry, was the respected leader of the Virginia delegation, he held several private meetings with him. Soon the Virginia and Massachusetts delegates were voting together on matters before the Congress.

On September 9, a convention held in Suffolk County, Massachusetts, which included Boston, passed a series of resolves. Paul Revere rode to Philadelphia in a record week's time and gave them to Samuel Adams who laid them before the Congress. He wrote, "They were read with great applause."

The Suffolk Resolves repeated the list of the colonies' grievances against Great Britain. They demanded a repeal of the Intolerable Acts, especially the closing of Boston Harbor; the new customs regulations; the quartering of troops in people's inns, eating houses, and other buildings; and the East India Tea Act. They urged Americans to train their militias, to stockpile weapons and supplies, and to prepare for war. They demanded that steps be taken to hurt Great Britain economically. The Suffolk Resolves stated that each colony's assembly had the right to draw up its own laws except on trade with other countries. The Congress endorsed, that is, approved of, the Suffolk Resolves. It then began work on its own Declaration of Rights and Grievances, which it adopted on October 14, 1774. The Congress pledged to come to the aid of Massachusetts if it was attacked.

Then Richard Henry Lee of Virginia proposed that a Continental Association be formed. No British merchandise would be imported after December 1, 1774. Nor would the colonies import enslaved people after that date. After March 1, 1775, people would neither buy nor use tea or other British goods that were not supposed to be imported. After September 1, 1775, nothing would be exported to Great Britain or its other colonies. Committees would be appointed in all counties, cities, and towns to enforce this agreement. These committees would be given the power to seize the stock of any merchant who traded with Great Britain. It was also agreed that the colonies would not trade or do business with any colony not agreeing with the Continental Association. The delegates hoped their show of unity would force Britain to return their liberties or face the ruin of its economy.

The First Continental Congress adjourned on October 26, 1774. A final resolution had been passed to meet on May 10, 1775, if the rights and liberties of the colonies had not been fully restored.

Samuel and John Adams returned to Boston in late November. They found anarchy, complete disorder. The Sons of Liberty controlled almost all of Massachusetts. Only Boston and its troops and warships remained under General Gage's control. He had been forced to move the capital back to Boston from Salem. Tories rushed to Boston for protection under General Gage and his soldiers. Whigs were leaving Boston to get away from the soldiers. There were no courts, no Council, no House of Representatives. No taxes were collected, so there was no money to run the colony. In desperation, the elected representatives had convened in Concord as a Provincial Congress with John Hancock as their president. It was not legal under the charter or any other law. The delegates pledged allegiance to the king while they passed resolutions providing for an army of 15,000 men plus cannons, mortars, and ammunition. Hancock was chosen to head a Committee of Public Safety with the power to call the militia into action. The Minutemen, special units of the militia, pledged to fight at a moment's notice. Meanwhile, General Gage was importing more troops all the time.

Matters were so bad, one word from Adams and the war would have started then and there. Yet Adams counseled patience. The time for an armed uprising was not yet right. Although the other colonies had pledged to come to the aid of Massachusetts, it was only under the condition that Massachusetts was attacked. He would wait for another British blunder to enrage everyone. He did not have to wait long.

In early 1775, Parliament passed a declaration proclaiming a state of rebellion in Massachusetts. The king commanded all powder and arms be seized. Gage was urged to strike, to show authority, and to arrest rebel leaders. Gage drew up a list of those patriot leaders to arrest if fighting started. London and Tory newspapers said Adams and Hancock would soon be hanged. Their families pleaded with them to leave Boston. Finally, they moved to the home of Adams's father-in-law in Cambridge.

They left there to attend another meeting of the Provincial Congress in Concord. When it adjourned on April 15, the two men decided not to return to Cambridge but to go to Hancock's grandfather's house in nearby Lexington. The house was now occupied by Jonas Clarke, Lexington's minister, who was a relation of Hancock's. On Sunday, April 16, Paul Revere rode out from Boston to give them disturbing news. Patriot spies had noticed a change in the British soldiers' routine. Also, the lifeboats usually kept aboard the royal navy ships in Boston Harbor had been put into the water. This could only mean General Gage was going to attack. But where? Worcester or Marblehead, which had large caches of arms? Adams, Hancock, and Revere thought the munitions and supplies hidden at Concord were a likely target. Revere was urged to warn Concord so the patriots there could move or hide the arms.

On Monday and Tuesday, people kept coming to the Clarke house with warnings and scraps of information. A guard of Minutemen was posted to protect Adams and Hancock. At midnight, Paul Revere galloped up on an exhausted horse shouting, "The Regulars are out!" Sergeant Monroe, in charge of the Minutemen guarding the house, told Revere to be quiet. Everyone had gone to bed and did not want to be disturbed by any noise.

John Hancock, who was not yet asleep, recognized Revere's voice and roused everyone. Paul Revere told them he had seen more than 1,000 troops being rowed across the Charles River a few hours before. He was sure their destination was Lexington where they intended to arrest Samuel Adams and John Hancock. Then they would go on to Concord and seize the arms there. Half an hour later William Dawes, the other messenger sent out from Boston, arrived and gave the same story.

Revere and Dawes left to ride to Concord, warning Minutemen as they went. By one o'clock in the morning, Captain John Parker and 30 Minutemen had assembled on Lexington Green to await the arrival of the troops.

Inside the Clarke house a battle was already in progress. John Hancock was cleaning his gun, determined to join Captain Parker and fight the redcoats. Adams insisted that Hancock's fighting would be an act of foolish bravado. To stand with the Minutemen meant death or capture. Hancock was to take James Bowdoin's place as a delegate to the Second Continental Congress, and he must come to Philadelphia with Adams. The master persuader finally won. At dawn, the Hancock carriage rumbled out of Lexington headed north to Woburn. It went across open fields to avoid any British spies watching the roads.

Paul Revere, who had been captured by the British on the road to Concord and then released, went with the two men. After a few miles, Hancock remembered he had forgotten a trunk full of important papers that must not fall into British hands. Revere went back to Lexington to hide it.

By breakfast time on Wednesday morning April 19, hundreds of British troops led by Major John Pitcairn reached Lexington.

Revere rode to Lexington to warn Hancock and Adams that the British were coming. He was captured while riding to Concord.

The 77 Minutemen, wearing arm bands for identification, faced them. Pitcairn charged his men not to fire and told the Minutemen to disperse. Captain Parker's orders to his men became famous. "Stand your ground. Don't fire unless fired upon, but if they mean to have a war let it begin here!"

Someone, however, did fire. It has never been determined where that shot came from, but it started the American Revolution. More shots were fired by both sides. Within seconds, eight Americans lay dead on Lexington Green. Ten more were wounded.

As they bumped over the fields, Adams and Hancock could hear the sound of gunfire. Samuel Adams remarked, "O! what a glorious morning is this!" Hancock supposedly said later that at first he had thought Adams was talking about the weather.

The pair of patriots went to Worcester where they were to meet John Adams, Thomas Cushing, and Robert Treat Paine. But these three men were not there. Adams and Hancock were desperate for news. They did not know that church bells had rung from village to village alerting the Minutemen. Word of the killings at Lexington spread like wildfire. When the British tried to

At the April 19, 1775, Battle of Lexington, eight Americans and one British soldier were killed. The Revolutionary War had begun.

march across the North Bridge at Concord, hundreds of Minutemen fired on them. The British retreated. Minutemen followed them, firing from behind trees and rocks and barns. By the time the British soldiers reached the safety of Boston again, 73 were dead, 179 wounded, and 21 missing. Ninety-five Americans were lost that day.

After waiting three days, Adams and Hancock set out for Philadelphia, fearing their three fellow delegates had been taken prisoner by Gage. On the road to New York, they heard the pounding of horses' hooves. Samuel Adams turned to look back and recognized the pudgy, round face of his cousin John followed by Cushing and Paine. They had had to sneak out of Boston one at a time, but they made it.

On May 10, 1775, the Second Continental Congress met. Nothing much had changed. Most of the members were still reluctant to adopt complete independence. There were two new members besides Hancock—Thomas Jefferson and Benjamin Franklin, who had returned from England only three days before. On May 24, Hancock was elected president of the Continental Congress.

On the same day the Continental Congress met, Ethan Allen and Benedict Arnold, with soldiers from the Green Mountains of the New Hampshire colony, captured Fort Ticonderoga on Lake Champlain. Not a single life was lost on either side. This little army then swept on to Canada capturing Montreal and laying siege to Quebec for almost a year.

Samuel Adams had long advocated that local militias in every town and hamlet of Massachusetts prepare to fight for their liberties. Now there were 16,000 of those men outside Boston with no leadership.

He encouraged Congress to make the Massachusetts militia and the Green Mountain Boys their army and appoint a commander-in-chief to raise a large army from all the colonies. This was a hard thing for Adams to do, for he at first thought militias could do the job if it came to fighting the British. He feared the tyranny that could come from a large standing army. But eventually he came to see it was the only way to win. John Adams nominated George Washington as commander-in-chief, and Samuel

Adams seconded the nomination. John Hancock, sitting at the president's desk, was visibly disappointed. He thought he should have the job because he had sacrificed so much for the cause. But aside from commanding the ceremonial Boston cadets, he had no military experience. Hancock never forgave the Adamses.

Before General Washington could reach Boston, the Massachusetts militia fortified Breed's Hill in Charlestown. The British sent 2,300 trained troops led by Major John Pitcairn to dislodge the 1,600 Americans on June 17. Twice the redcoats charged up the hill only to be driven back. If the Americans had not run out of ammunition, they would have won the battle. They killed or wounded almost half of Pitcairn's men including Pitcairn himself. Obeying Colonel William Prescott's orders, the Americans did not fire until they saw the whites of the redcoats' eyes. Four hundred Americans were killed or wounded at the Battle of Bunker Hill (which was actually fought at Breed's Hill).

General Gage offered amnesty to those in Massachusetts who would lay down their arms and swear allegiance to the king—all except Samuel Adams and John Hancock. They were branded traitors. Their property was seized. Betsy Adams and Sam's daughter Hannah had to flee to Cambridge.

Despite Lexington, Concord, and Bunker Hill, Congress would only write another petition to the king. It asked again for reconciliation and restoration of the colonists' rights. King George III's answer was to declare the colonies in a state of open rebellion. He also ordered the blockade of all American ports.

On the same day this news of the king's vengeance reached Philadelphia, a pamphlet entitled *Common Sense* written by Thomas Paine appeared in the bookstalls of Philadelphia. It was addressed to ordinary people so that even those with a simple dame school education could understand it. *Common Sense* attacked the whole idea of people being ruled by kings and queens. It declared, "Of more worth is one honest man to society and in the sight of God, than all the crowned ruffians that ever lived." The pamphlet glorified independence. "The sun never shined on a cause of greater Worth," and it ridiculed the idea of the continent of North America being ruled by the island of Great Britain. *Common Sense* electrified the colonies.

Even after *Common Sense,* Congress would not unanimously vote for independence. Instead the delegates talked, talked, talked. Samuel Adams became so frustrated he threatened that the New England states would become independent by themselves. He already had secret agreements between the four colonies of Massachusetts, Connecticut, New Hampshire, and Rhode Island that they would combine their militias into one army. But Benjamin Franklin talked Adams out of it. New England could not stand alone against England, he reasoned.

Congress did send Silas Deane, a lawyer and delegate from Connecticut, to Europe to beg or buy guns, ammunition, clothing, and blankets for Washington's army. Not enough could be manufactured in the colonies. A marine committee headed by John Hancock was set up to start building 13 frigates with 24 to 32 guns each. Nobody knew more about Atlantic shipping than Hancock. Samuel Adams started calling the colonies "states" and the king "the tyrant." He urged states to set up their own governments and elect new officials to replace royal officials.

Samuel Adams talked to one delegate at a time, trying to convince each one to come out for independence. John and Samuel Adams made themselves unpopular by accusing every man who was not in favor of independence of being a traitor. Samuel Adams had seen to it that his old friend Thomas Cushing was not elected for another term in the Congress because he wavered on the independence issue. Elbridge Gerry, who favored independence, replaced him. Samuel Adams tried to manage the Congress the way he had the Boston Caucus, the town meetings, and the Massachusetts House of Representatives. But he was dealing with some of the best and brightest men in America. They did not trust him. John and Samuel Adams, that "brace of Adamses," were not put on important congressional committees for a time.

General Washington had cannons dragged over the mountains all the way from Fort Ticonderoga to the Boston area. On March 1, 1776, he had them set up on Dorchester Heights overlooking Boston. This put all of Boston and the ships in the harbor under American guns. General William Howe, who had replaced General Gage as commander-in-chief of the British Army in

North America, knew his situation was hopeless. He evacuated the town. All the soldiers and 1,100 Tories sailed on 170 ships to Halifax, Nova Scotia, in Canada. Boston was free at last. Adams wrote to a friend in Boston:

> I heartily congratulate you upon the sudden and important Change of our Affairs in the Removal of the Barbarians from the Capital. . . . I hope we shall be upon our Guard against future Attempts. Will not Care be taken immediately to fortify the Harbour & thereby prevent the Entrance of Ships of War ever hereafter?

In April of 1776, North Carolina declared for independence. Massachusetts already had. Virginia followed, then Maryland. On June 5, Richard Henry Lee of Virginia introduced a resolution to the Congress. "These united colonies are, and of right ought to be, free and independent states; that they are absolved from all

General George Washington watches the British evacuate Boston. The British troopships sailed to Halifax, Nova Scotia.

The Declaration of Independence was signed by members of Congress. Samuel Adams was the ninth delegate to sign it.

allegiance to the British Crown; and that all political connection between them and the State of Great Britain is, and ought to be, totally dissolved." There it was. Independence. The delegates to the Second Continental Congress must at last decide.

The debate went on for five days. On the last day, Samuel Adams gave a long speech, with many points on why the colonies should be independent. He said, "If there is any man so base, or so weak as to prefer a dependence on Great Britain to the dignity and happiness of living a member of *a free and independent nation*, let me tell him that *necessity* now demands what the generous principles of patriotism should have dictated." It convinced a few more delegates. John Adams proposed three committees be set up: One to write a declaration of independence; the second, a secret committee on correspondence, to get foreign aid from Great Britain's

91

enemies, France and Spain. The third committee would draw up a plan to govern once independence was declared. John Adams, along with Thomas Jefferson, Robert Livingston of New York, Roger Sherman of Connecticut, and Benjamin Franklin, drew up the Declaration of Independence. Jefferson did most of the writing. John Adams was also on the secret committee for foreign alliances.

Samuel Adams was put on the committee to draw up the Articles of Confederation, the plan for governing, but he did not work at it. Instead, he strongly persuaded wavering delegates to vote for independence. When Congress met again on July 1, only four states did not come out for independence. The vote was put off until July 2 when every sentence in the proposed declaration of independence was analyzed and discussed. Although nine states were enough to pass it, Samuel Adams wanted a unanimous vote. Delaware changed its vote. So did Pennsylvania. South Carolina gave in. New York abstained, awaiting instructions and did not vote to make it unanimous until July 15.

On July 4, "The Unanimous Declaration of the Thirteen United States of America" having been approved by 12 of the states, and thus not really unanimous at that date, was signed by John Hancock as president of the Congress. Fifty members wrote their names on a handsomely embossed official copy on August 2, 1776. John Adams was the sixth man to sign; Samuel Adams was the ninth.

CHAPTER NINE

The Grim Years

What Samuel Adams had worked and sacrificed for, had come to pass. His impossible dream had become a reality. The Fourth of July, 1776, should have been the happiest day in Samuel Adams's life.

But it wasn't. He wrote to a friend a few days later:

> The Congress has at length declared the Colonies free and independent States. . . . Much I am affraid has been lost by delaying to take this decisive Step. It is my opinion that if it had been done Nine months ago . . . Canada would [by] this time have been one of the United Colonies; but "Much is to be endurd for the hardness of Mens hearts." We shall now see the Way clear to form a Confederation, contract Alliances & send Embassadors to foreign Powers & do other Acts becoming the Character we have assumd. [original spelling and punctuation]

The Declaration of Independence led to many more problems than it solved. The people were not ready for independence. Perhaps as much as a quarter or a third of the population—the Tories—was sympathetic to the enemy. These people now called themselves Loyalists, meaning loyal to Great Britain. Even among the non-Tories there was no great feeling of unity.

The former colonies still did not trust one another. It was agreed that the United States of America would be a confederation of states with a weak central government. Yet it took almost a year and a half for the Articles of Confederation to be passed by Congress and accepted by 12 states. The 13th state, Maryland, refused to sign it until 1781, five years after the Declaration of Independence. The new United States of America had no real

Samuel Adams. This engraving was made by Paul Revere.

organized constitutional government for that long a time.

Nevertheless, the Congress plunged ahead without any legal power granted by any piece of paper, vote of the people, or even tradition. What choice did they have? Great Britain was not about to let its profitable colonies go quietly. American delegates who had originally met to protest now had to organize and govern a new country and at the same time fight an all-out war against the world's strongest power.

On July 5, 1776, Samuel Adams proposed that American ambassadors be sent to foreign countries. Soon Benjamin Franklin of Pennsylvania and Arthur Lee of Virginia were on their way to Europe to join Silas Deane of Connecticut in the search for financial and military assistance. To keep their independence, the new United States had to have help from Great Britain's traditional enemies—France, Spain, and the Netherlands. The Americans could raise enough men to fight the British, but they had no money. Congress began printing money with no backing of gold or silver; it didn't even have the backing of land as Deacon Adams's Land Bank of 1740 once had. Inflation soared.

The army and navy were placed strictly under the control of Congress. Samuel and John Adams were appointed to the military committee, and Samuel Adams made himself chairman of the Committee on the State of the Northern Army. He knew nothing of military affairs. He had not fought in the French and Indian

War when he was a young man. Nor did he ever serve a day in the Massachusetts militia. But that did not stop him from meddling in military affairs. Adams, without consulting Washington, appointed generals—bad ones like Charles Lee and good ones like Friedrich von Steuben. At the same time, he and his cousin John worked tirelessly to support Washington's army with men, munitions, and money. To induce men to enlist for the duration of the war, not just three months at a time, Samuel Adams wanted to offer bonuses of 100 acres of land and some cash. He was willing to do almost anything, for the military situation was bad.

The Americans under Benedict Arnold had been driven from Canada, losing Montreal and eventually Fort Ticonderoga in New York State. In August of 1776, the British general William Howe, who had fled Boston the year before, returned to the New York City area from Halifax with more troops. His brother, Admiral Richard Howe, arrived with the British fleet and with soldiers hired from German states. By the end of August, they had won the Battle of Long Island. Washington had to abandon New York City to them, first retreating to Fort Washington on Harlem Heights at the north end of Manhattan Island. But this, too, fell. Fort Lee across the Hudson River was soon overrun. Washington and his troops had to flee across New Jersey in December to the Pennsylvania side of the Delaware River. By that time, he had scarcely 1,000 men left in his army, and their enlistments were due to be up December 31, 1776.

Through it all, Samuel Adams continued to be optimistic. In the darkest days of that December he wrote to his wife, Betsy:

> I am still in good Health and Spirits, although the Enemy is within Forty Miles of this City [Philadelphia]. I do not regret the Part I have taken in a Cause so just and interesting to Mankind. I must confess it chagrins me greatly to find it so illy supported by the People of Pennsylvania and the Jerseys. They seem to me to be determined to give it up—but I trust that my dear New England will maintain it at the Expense of every thing dear to them in this Life— they know how to prize their Liberties. May Heaven

bless them! . . . If this City should be *surrendered*, I should by no means despair of our Cause. It is a righteous Cause and I am fully perswaded righteous Heaven will succeed it.

To the discouraged and frightened American people, he issued a report saying the army was being reorganized and reinforced. Privateers, armed private ships licensed to attack enemy shipping, were taking a huge toll of British shipping. One wonders what the people thought when on December 12, 1776, the Congress was so afraid the British would soon overrun Philadelphia that they voted to flee to Baltimore. In those desperate times, Samuel Adams, of all people, proposed that General Washington be granted full powers to conduct the war as he saw fit. Adams did the one thing he had feared most. He favored giving a general the power to become a dictator or even a king with an army to back him up. But Adams trusted Washington with his dedication to the cause and his strong character to use his power wisely. Adams was not disappointed.

It was Thomas Paine who came to the rescue again. A major in the army, he had been with Washington on the retreat across New Jersey. He published a pamphlet he called the *American Crisis* to give people courage. "These are the times that try men's souls. The Summer soldier and the sunshine patriot will, in this crisis, shrink from the service of his country; but he that stands it NOW deserves the love and thanks of man and woman."

Paine pointed to the dreadful alternative if the war failed, and he suggested what must be done to win. "I call not upon a few, but upon all, not on this state or that state, but on every state; up and help us."

Washington followed up the *Crisis* paper by a daring raid Christmas night at Trenton, New Jersey. With hardly a shot fired, 1,000 enemy troops surrendered. Washington successfully managed another surprise attack on Princeton a few days later. The country turned from despair to hope.

Congress moved back to Philadelphia from Baltimore on March 12, 1777. That same month the three commissioners in Europe—Franklin, Deane, and Lee—were successful in persuading France to give the United States a large loan of money for the duration of the war.

When the season for war resumed again in June of 1777, Washington knew he did not have enough military strength to take the offensive. General Howe kept him guessing all summer as to where he was going to attack. Then in August, Howe loaded his troops onto ships and headed for Chesapeake Bay to attack Philadelphia. There was no American navy to harass him. Washington could only march overland and prepare to meet Howe's attack at Brandywine Creek, a few miles southwest of Philadelphia. During the battle on September 11, 1777, the Americans were outmaneuvered, so they retreated to fight another day. As the British marched unopposed into Philadelphia, the Congress fled again. On October 4, Washington attacked at Germantown north of Philadelphia. But there was heavy fog, which led to great confusion, and the Americans lost the battle. Washington spent the next two months harassing the British, but accomplished little. He went into winter quarters at Valley Forge, Pennsylvania.

This time Congress moved all the way to York, Pennsylvania, safely on the other side of the broad Susquehanna River. It was so far away that only 15 to 20 members of Congress out of more than 50 bothered to show up. The Congress could do nothing to supply Washington at Valley Forge. Three thousand men froze to death. Smallpox broke out. In this rich farming land, the people refused to sell food to the Americans for paper money. Instead, they sold to the British in Philadelphia for hard money. Never was there a more discouraging time. Many people took the amnesty offered by the British.

Amid all Washington's failures, word came of a great American victory. British general John Burgoyne had been defeated at Saratoga, New York. Five thousand British troops surrendered to General Horatio Gates on October 17, 1777. The victory of General Gates at the Battle of Saratoga was a turning point in the war in several ways. It gave a huge boost to the morale of the American people and instilled some confidence in them that they could win. But it caused many people, especially in Congress, to lose confidence in General Washington. Congress was made up of nonmilitary men like the Adamses. They had no idea of military strategy, training, or discipline. Nor did they fully grasp the problems of logistics—how to feed, clothe, and shelter soldiers in the field or obtain and transport military supplies. They could only complain that Washington should be fighting harder. Why wasn't he going on the attack instead of suffering defeat after defeat? Yet he was given little help from Congress. Washington wrote dozens of letters every day to Congress and the states pleading for more help. Each state according to its size and population was supposed to provide Congress with money and supplies to support the Continental Army. But the states rarely met their assigned share of the costs.

With little to do in York, John Adams resigned from the Congress, and Samuel Adams requested leave to go home to Boston. They had not seen their families in over a year, and Samuel Adams had been ill since the Congress was in Baltimore. He walked with a cane and had fainted several times. The doctors warned him to stay in bed, but he would not. He had too much work to do. Hancock's health was also poor, and he, too, asked for a leave at this time. But the three Bostonians did not travel together. As president of the Congress, Hancock insisted that Washington give him 15 mounted soldiers to escort him.

In Boston, the Adams cousins found the Whigs were divided between Samuel Adams Whigs and John Hancock Whigs. The strict Puritan Samuel Adams openly criticized Hancock's expensive lifestyle, although he had not done so before in the years they were political allies. Hancock, once the political student of Samuel Adams, floated rumors that Adams was involved in the Conway Cabal. This was a plot of some congressmen and generals to replace Washington with General Horatio Gates, the hero of the Battle of Saratoga. People believed these accusations despite the fact that there was no proof that Adams had been part of the plot. Nevertheless, the Boston town meeting severely reprimanded him. Adams was forced into loudly defending himself and writing letter after letter of loyalty to Washington.

On the other hand, the people loved John Hancock. They believed he was a great patriot and that he spent his money for the public good. When Hancock made himself a major general of

This famous portrait of John Hancock was painted by John
Singleton Copley 11 years before the American Revolution.

99

the Massachusetts militia, most people thought no one deserved it more.

The fortunes of the new United States turned for the better in 1778. On February 6, the three American commissioners signed the Treaty of Alliance with France. France recognized the United States as an independent country. It pledged to send money, guns, military supplies, even troops, and its navy to attack the blockade the British had set up. In return, France hoped to regain at least part of Canada. It was a brilliant piece of diplomacy on the part of the Americans. That same month, John Adams was appointed to replace Silas Deane, who was called home to explain some irregular financial dealings.

The British abandoned Philadelphia in June of 1778, thinking the French fleet would soon be coming up the Delaware River. New York was easier for the British to defend. As the British forces marched across New Jersey, Washington attacked them. While at Valley Forge, Friedrich von Steuben, a former Prussian army officer, had taught the Americans the basics of how to be an army. They had learned their lessons well. The Americans would have won the Battle of Monmouth in late June 1778 if General Charles Lee had not disobeyed Washington's orders and retreated.

With the French helping the Americans, the British began to send out peace feelers. The Americans were not the easy victims they had thought they would be. However, the British price for peace was keeping the colonies as colonies. But by 1778, the Americans would settle for nothing less than recognition of their independence. Not only members of Congress felt this way; the people now backed them up. Samuel Adams sent a long open letter to the British peace commissioners who had come to negotiate with the Congress at York and been refused:

> Now, if you will take the poor advice of one who is really a friend to England & Englishmen . . . away with your fleets and your armies, acknowledge the independence of America; and as ambassadors, and not commissioners, solicit a treaty of peace, amity, commerce, and alliance with the rising States of this Western World.

In July of 1778, Congress returned to Philadelphia a second time. By early 1779, Adams was ill again. He tried to resign from Congress, but the Massachusetts General Court would not accept his resignation. He was too important. With his small salary further reduced by inflation, he could not support himself, his wife, and his daughter no matter how cheaply he tried to live in Philadelphia. This further undermined his health. His fine clothes had grown shabby. Since he could not afford better ones, he started a propaganda campaign that to be threadbare showed one's patriotism. Therefore, it was fashionable to look the way he did.

Samuel Adams left Philadelphia in mid-June 1779, not to return for almost a year. When he reached Boston, he found his wife and daughter living in a confiscated Tory house on Milk Street. The Adams family home on Purchase Street had been occupied by the British during 1775 and early 1776. The inside had been destroyed, the fine furniture of Deacon Adams stolen or used for firewood. The Milk Street house was furnished from beds to pots and pans with secondhand things once belonging to Tories who had fled.

Not long after Samuel Adams reached Boston, a ship brought John Adams home from France. The two cousins went to work almost at once on the Massachusetts Constitution. A special constitutional convention had been elected to write a new constitution. Twelve men were designated to work on it. Of those, three did the work: Samuel and John Adams and James Bowdoin. John Adams drew up most of it. He based it on the old Massachusetts Charter. In the new Massachusetts Constitution there was a bill of rights, which the people demanded. Yet only property owners could vote. He feared women demanding a vote or boys under 21 or the drifters through town. He had seen the chaos of the town meeting taken over by the meaner sort with the biggest mouths and stoutest sticks. In John Adams's constitution, there were to be two parts to the legislative branch. The members of the lower House of Representatives would be elected from each town. It would serve all the people in general. The upper house, which became known as the Senate, would have only members who owned at least $1,000 worth of property. The constitution provided for a governor and a separate court system. The three parts would serve as a system of checks and balances. It reserved most rights for the state, as both Adamses were opposed to a strong central United States government.

But Samuel Adams disagreed with John Adams about part of the Massachusetts Constitution. He believed everyone should be allowed to vote, not just property owners. He also thought the state should provide every child with a free education.

Samuel Adams drew up the section on religion. It said if people did not have a church of their own, they had to pay taxes to support the Puritan Church. Every Christian branch or denomination not already in Massachusetts would not be allowed in. Despite protests against it, this bigoted article stayed in the Massachusetts Constitution for 50 years.

The Massachusetts Constitution was ratified in 1780. That fall John Hancock was elected the first governor—a job he felt was more important than being president of the Continental Congress. In the same election, Samuel Adams ran for the office of first secretary of the Commonwealth of Massachusetts and lost.

CHAPTER TEN

Governor Samuel Adams

Samuel Adams was not in Boston to face his rejection by the voters when he ran for the office of first secretary of the Commonwealth of Massachusetts. He had returned to Philadelphia and Congress in June 1780. The war was not going well despite the help of France—and of Spain, which had declared war on Great Britain in 1779. Much of the fighting had moved to the southern states. Savannah had been captured by the British. Georgia and South Carolina had been overrun. The Americans under capable generals—Nathaniel Greene, Daniel Morgan, Thomas Sumter, and Horatio Gates—fought hard. What gains the Americans made were in guerrilla fighting, acting in small, independent units that carried out harassment, sabotage, and swift hit-and-run attacks. The British still had not learned this way of fighting, which was called "Indian"-style.

The United States Treasury was near bankruptcy. Some soldiers mutinied because they had not been paid. Taxpayers protested loudly. In early 1781, Thomas Paine and Colonel John Laurens, an aide to General Washington, went to France and secured two ships of supplies and $5 million. It helped, but so much more was needed.

Samuel Adams worked tirelessly to make the states give their fair share of support to the army. He wrote to Richard Henry Lee:

> My friend, we must not suffer anything to discourage us in this great conflict. . . . It is our duty to make every proper exertion in our respective States to revive the old patriotic feelings among the people at large, and to get the public departments, especially the most important of them, filled with men of understanding and inflexible virtue.

But this great effort took its toll on Adams. When he thought he could no longer carry on, he wrote to the president of the Massachusetts Senate:

> Philadelphia, 13th March, 1781.
>
> SIR,—
>
> I beg the favor of you to communicate to the General Assembly my wish to return home as early as may be; and to request that I may be relieved by one of my colleagues, or in such manner as shall be thought most proper.
>
> I flatter myself I shall be excused in making this request, from a consideration of the length of time since I last left Massachusetts, and that I am apprehensive my health will not admit of my spending another summer in this city.
>
> I am, with every sentiment of duty and respect to the Assembly, sir, your most obedient and very humble servant,
>
> SAMUEL ADAMS.

A tired and sick Samuel Adams reached Boston in April. He had no income, so his friends saw to it that he was elected to fill a vacant seat in the new Massachusetts Senate. Where he got the $1,000 to qualify, no one knows. Soon he was elected president of that body. This position paid him a salary that he needed worse than ever. He had to support his wife, daughter, and son. His son had graduated from Harvard and become a doctor in Boston. When the Revolution had started, he had served as a surgeon in the army. But the hardships of camp life had broken his own health, and he was unable to practice his profession.

Two months after Adams's return, his daughter, Hannah, married Captain Thomas Wells, the younger brother of her stepmother, Betsy. Although it was a quiet ceremony in the Puritan tradition, even John Hancock came to the wedding.

Instead of constantly going to political meetings or dining with gentleman friends as he had in the past, Adams stayed at home with his family. Yet sometimes he visited the tough waterfront taverns again. He seemed to have genuinely liked the people there who were so unlike himself. Perhaps he did not want them to think he would ever forget about those who had been among the first to support him in the early days.

By the middle of 1781, the tide of the war finally turned. The Continental Army had recaptured the southern states except for three major ports. In October, General Washington and his army of about 9,000 American troops, with the help of 7,800 French soldiers and the French fleet, lay siege to a large British force at Yorktown, Virginia. On October 19, 8,000 British soldiers and sailors, one-fourth of all in North America, surrendered. Most of the American people, including the leaders in the states and members of the Congress, thought the war was over. They ignored the king's speech insisting that he was determined to fight on. General Washington warned in hundreds of letters that the war could still be lost because fighting continued.

The surrender at Yorktown brought about the resignation of the British prime minister Lord North, who had once vowed to see America prostrate at the king's feet. The British people were tired of war, too. On February 27, 1782, Parliament voted to start peace talks. King George was so angry he threatened to abdicate. In September, John Adams, John Jay, and Benjamin Franklin began formal peace negotiations in Paris, France. By November 30, 1782, a preliminary peace treaty was signed, and the official Treaty of Paris was signed on September 3, 1783.

After the war, Boston, indeed all of Massachusetts, was a sorry place. The state suffered terribly from a severe depression lasting from 1784 through 1788. The peace treaty forbade American ships to trade in the British ports of the West Indies. Most Boston-based ships had been lost to privateering during the war anyway. Shipyards and ropewalks were closed, laborers were out of work. Some returning soldiers who had suffered so much for the cause of independence were arrested for not being able to pay their creditors and were thrown into debtors' prison.

But many of those who had stayed safely at home and profited from the war were rich. They bought up the British and French goods that flooded into Boston and put them into grand old Tory houses. Adams feared all that had been gained in the long struggle would be lost. He had wanted the revolution so people would return to the Puritan ways of earlier times. It had been the basic reason behind all his activities for decades. He blamed the British for sending over their "fripperies" and "baubles" to undermine Puritan morals. After the war, he tried to get another nonimportation agreement. He scolded, "I love the people of Boston. I once thought that city would be the Christian Sparta. But alas! will men never be free? They will be free no longer than while they remain virtuous." But nobody listened.

There began to be outbreaks of violence among owners of small farms and businesses in rural areas over the high taxes being collected by the states to pay war debts. In 1786, the farmers of western Massachusetts were having the land they had wrested from the wilderness and had fought the Native Americans for taken away from them when they could not pay these taxes. Finally, they prevented the courts from foreclosing on their farms by taking up arms and crying "Liberty!" Their leader was a veteran of the Battle of Bunker Hill, Daniel Shays.

Samuel Adams saw the danger of civil war in what Shays was doing because he remembered what he himself had been like 20 years before. He knew this mob threatened his republic. One would have thought Adams, of all people, would have been in favor of people rebelling when their liberties were threatened. Instead, Samuel Adams thundered that no one should revolt against the laws of a republic because they had a voice in making those laws. He asked the governor to call out the militia and crush the rebellion. When Shays and the other leaders were captured, Adams had no sympathy for them. He thought they should all hang. But Governor Hancock saw that would only cause more trouble and pardoned them all. This made Hancock even more popular.

Shays's Rebellion was just one of many proofs that the Articles of Confederation was not working. Each state acted like an independent country, printing its own money, even putting up tariffs against other states' products. It was decided that each state should send delegates to a convention to meet in Philadelphia in May of 1787 to revise the Articles of Confederation. Only Rhode Island did not send delegates. The men soon realized the Articles could never be revised to meet the needs of the United States. After four months of compromise, the delegates worked out a remarkable form of government never before seen on this earth. Much of it was based on the Massachusetts Constitution of 1780 written by John Adams. They called it simply the United States Constitution. Thirty-nine delegates signed it on September 17, 1787. George Washington's name was first. But neither John Adams nor Samuel Adams was among the delegates who had written it. By this time, John Adams was the United States ambassador to Great Britain. Samuel Adams had failed to be elected a delegate.

Shays's Rebellion. Daniel Shays's force of about 1,200 men attacked a government arsenal at Springfield, Massachusetts.

Nine of the 13 states had to ratify, that is, approve, the Constitution before it could be put into effect. In December, Delaware was the first state to ratify it.

On January 9, 1788, the Massachusetts Constitutional Convention met in Boston for the purpose of approving or rejecting the document. John Hancock was elected president of the gathering. Both he and Samuel Adams were undecided about whether to vote for it or against it. Patrick Henry and Richard Henry Lee of Virginia were against it, as was Elbridge Gerry of Massachusetts. These were all men who, in the past, had sided with Samuel Adams. They thought the new Constitution did not protect individual liberties. Disagreement over the new Constitution caused the rise of two opposing parties in the United States. The Federalists favored adoption of the new Constitution. The Anti-Federalists objected because it gave the central government too much power.

In Boston, men like Paul Revere and other craftsmen, artisans, and small-business men strongly supported the new Constitution. Only when a large delegation of them led by Revere called upon Samuel Adams and convinced him of their views did he reluctantly decide to vote for it. But he still held out until the Massachusetts Constitutional Convention agreed to recommend that the protection of some rights such as trial by jury be added to the Constitution. Even then he had his doubts. A year later, he wrote to Richard Henry Lee, "I hope the federal Congress is vested with [legally given] Powers adequate to all the great purposes of the federal Union; . . . The Powers vested in Government by the People, the only just Source of such Powers, ought to be critically defined and well understood."

Hancock was won over by promises of support from Federalists to become the first President of the United States. Still, approval of the new Constitution was by a majority of only 19 votes in Massachusetts. At least nine states had to ratify the Constitution before it could go into effect. In June 1788, New Hampshire became the ninth state. The Constitution had been officially ratified, and plans were made to hold the first elections in early 1789. North Carolina and Rhode Island held out the longest—until 1789 and 1790—refusing to ratify the Constitution until they were assured that a Bill of Rights would eventually be added. A Bill of Rights would guarantee rights, such as freedom of religion and freedom of the press. On December 15, 1791, the new Congress did add a Bill of Rights to the Constitution after the new government had been functioning for about three years.

Samuel Adams was persuaded to run for the new Congress, but as neither a Federalist nor an Anti-Federalist. He would not stoop to campaign, and he was defeated by Fisher Ames, a 31-year-old Federalist candidate. A new generation was taking over.

Adams suffered another loss far more dear to him. In the midst of the Constitutional Convention his son, Dr. Samuel Adams, died suddenly at the age of 37. Ironically, the loss of his son resulted in Adams finally becoming financially secure. Never having married, Dr. Adams's back wages due him for his services as an army surgeon were paid to his father—some $5,000. For once in his life, Adams made a good financial investment. He bought the Peacock Tavern and 40 acres of land in Jamaica Plain outside Boston. The income from this property was $1,000 a year.

John Adams returned from Europe in 1788. Ten months later, when Washington was elected U.S. President unanimously, crushing the hopes of Hancock, John Adams was elected Vice-President. A northerner and a southerner headed the United States, which pleased most people. They were sworn in on April 30, 1789, in New York City, the new capital of the United States.

That same year John Hancock and Samuel Adams, who had patched up their differences, were elected governor and lieutenant governor of Massachusetts. Political ideas did not separate them as they ran neither as Federalist nor Anti-Federalist. They were a well liked and familiar team. The people reelected them every year. When John Hancock died in 1793, Samuel Adams became governor. The next year, he was elected governor in his own right. Although he was 72 years old, he seemed to have regained his health and worked 12 hours a day. Each year he became more and more popular until nobody bothered to oppose him in elections. This gave him great power to govern his Massachusetts as he pleased.

Adams had a blind spot about Tories. Exiled Tories who had managed to get to London often became merchants who sent those "fripperies" to Boston. Adams viewed them darkly as British agents who would take the Americans' cash as had happened during the Land Bank days of the early 1740s. Even those Tories who had sworn allegiance to the new United States he would not believe. He would not allow them to return; he would not allow them to be paid for their lost property; he would not even allow them to collect debts owed them from before the war. He sincerely thought their intent was to undermine the weak new nation. Adams continued to guard the door against any threat he saw to the hard-won liberties.

His hatred of Great Britain caused him to side with the Anti-Federalists finally. Another matter that split the two parties was the French Revolution, which had started in 1789. At first the French revolutionaries reduced the power of the French king and set up a constitutional government. But the French Revolution was not like the American Revolution. It was much bloodier. In 1793, the French king was executed. The Reign of Terror in France resulted in the execution of thousands of men, women, and even children. Yet Adams and the Anti-Federalists continued to support France and its foreign policy of opposing monarchies in Europe. The Federalists, who included Washington and John Adams, wanted the United States to remain neutral in revolutionary France's current war with Great Britain. President George Washington did not want to get into another war. The United States was still too powerless. France thought the United States should keep its promise made in the 1778 Treaty of Alliance and fight on France's side.

Adams and the Anti-Federalists were angry that Great Britain continued to stop and search American merchant ships on the high seas. The British pretext was that they were looking for deserters or goods being sent to its enemy France. They even kidnapped American sailors and forced them to serve in the British Navy. Great Britain continued to keep its West Indies ports closed to American ships, which hurt Boston. In addition, Great Britain refused to evacuate the Northwest military forts, although it had promised to do so in the 1783 peace treaty with the United States. These high-handed actions by Great Britain brought the United States to the brink of war. John Jay, chief justice of the United

States, negotiated a new treaty with Great Britain in 1794, but its terms were not good for the United States. Although Great Britain promised to leave the forts on U.S. land, the treaty still allowed restrictions on West Indies trade. There was rioting against it in Boston. Governor Adams refused to call out the state militia to stop it, for he opposed the treaty, too. He warned the public in a letter to the newspapers:

> I may never hereafter have an opportunity of publicly expressing my opinion on the Treaty made with the Court of London. I am therefore constrained with all due respect to our Constituted Authority to declare, that the Treaty appears to me to be pregnant with evil. It controuls some of the powers specially vested in Congress for the security of the people; and I fear that it may restore to Great Britain such an influence over the Government and people of this country as may not be consistent with the general welfare.

Reluctantly, the U.S. Senate approved the treaty in 1795, and President Washington just as reluctantly signed it. The agreement avoided war in the mid 1790s, but the problems it failed to solve would lead to the War of 1812.

In 1798, Washington said two terms were enough for any President and refused to run again. Some of Samuel Adams's friends wanted him to run for President. But at 76, he insisted he was too old. Nevertheless, he was nominated. John Adams received the most votes and became the second President of the United States. Thomas Jefferson had the second highest number so he became Vice-President. Samuel Adams came in fifth. He could have had a post in the cabinet, a group of the President's special advisers and department heads, but again he felt he was too old.

In January of 1797, the elderly Samuel Adams spoke before the Massachusetts Assembly. At the end of his speech he announced his retirement from public life. "The infirmities of age render me an unfit person in my own opinion, and very probably

John Adams served as President of the United States from 1797 to 1801.

in the opinion of others, to continue in this station."

Although he kept up a constant flow of letters to people, his shaking hand could no longer hold a pen. His grandchildren often wrote while he dictated. He seldom left his house on Winter Street. When he did go out, parents pointed him out to their children as the grandfather of his country. People continued to call upon him and ask his advice.

On Sunday morning, October 2, 1803, the bells of Boston began to toll, for Samuel Adams had died. Three days later he was given a grand state funeral, although he had requested just a

Samuel Adams was governor of Massachusetts from 1794 to 1797.

simple Puritan one. At Old Granary Burying Ground, Samuel Adams was laid to rest among the old Puritans he had patterned his life after. Out in Boston Harbor, the guns on Castle Island, now called Fort Independence, boomed in final salute.

> I thank God that I have lived to see my country independent and free. She may long enjoy her independence and freedom if she will. It depends on her virtue. She has gained the glorious prize, and it is my most fervent wish . . . that she may value and improve it as she ought.
>
> SAMUEL ADAMS

KEY DATES

1722	Samuel Adams is born on September 16 to Samuel and Mary Adams in Boston.
1729	Adams starts Boston Latin School.
1736	Adams enters Harvard College to study for the ministry.
1740	Adams earns his bachelor's degree.
1741	Adams's father's Land Bank is closed by Parliament. The Boston sheriff tries to seize his estate.
1743	Adams earns his master's degree from Harvard.
1747	Adams forms a political club and publishes a weekly newspaper, *The Public Advertizer*.
1748	Adams's father dies.
1749	Adams marries Elizabeth Checkley.
1756	Adams is elected a tax collector of Boston.
1757	Adams's wife dies leaving two children.
1758	The Boston sheriff again tries to seize Adams's property.
1764	Adams marries Elizabeth Wells.
1765	Adams's tax accounts found short; the Stamp Act passed by Parliament; Adams founds the Sons of Liberty; mob destroys Lt. Governor Hutchinson's house; Adams is elected to the Massachusetts House of Representatives.
1766	The Stamp Act is repealed by Parliament; Adams is elected clerk of the Massachusetts House of Representatives.
1767	The Townshend Acts are passed by Parliament.

1768	Adams writes the Massachusetts Circular Letter to other colonies; British troops occupy Boston.
1769	Governor Bernard is forced to leave Boston; Adams is in charge of Boston after near-fatal beating of his friend James Otis Junior.
1770	Boston Massacre takes place; Adams forces Lt. Governor Hutchinson to remove all troops from Boston; the Townshend Acts are repealed; Adams forms the first Committee of Correspondence.
1771	Adams begins to lose some of his political power.
1773	The East India Tea Act is passed by Parliament; secret letters of Hutchinson are sent by Franklin to Boston; Adams writes to the king for recall of Hutchinson; the Boston Tea Party takes place.
1774	Parliament passes the Intolerable Acts (Coercive Acts) ; Adams's old enemy Hutchinson leaves Boston; the port of Boston is closed; Adams is named delegate to the First Continental Congress; Adams presents Suffolk Resolves to Congress.
1775	Parliament declares Massachusetts in a state of rebellion; Adams ordered arrested; Adams escapes just before Battle of Lexington; Adams is a delegate to the Second Continental Congress.
1776	Adams wants to form New England colonies into an independent country; Washington drives British from Boston; Adams is ninth man to sign Declaration of Independence; Adams is put on congressional military committees; Adams recommends giving all power to General Washington as Congress flees Philadelphia.
1777	Adams is accused of being part of Conway Cabal; Congress again flees Philadelphia, this time for York, Pennsylvania.

1778	The French Treaty of Alliance is signed; the British leave Philadelphia.
1779	Samuel and John Adams write Massachusetts Constitution.
1780	Adams is defeated in election for secretary of the Commonwealth of Massachusetts.
1781	Adams resigns from Congress.
1783	Peace treaty ending the Revolutionary War is signed.
1788	Adams votes for the new U.S. Constitution; Adams's only son dies; Adams is defeated for a seat in the new Congress.
1789	Adams is elected lieutenant governor of Massachusetts.
1793	Adams becomes governor of Massachusetts when John Hancock dies.
1794	Adams is elected governor of Massachusetts in his own right.
1795	Adams is nominated as candidate for President and comes in fifth in the elections.
1797	Adams retires.
1803	Adams dies on October 2, in Boston.

amnesty A general pardon granted by a ruler or government to a large group of people guilty of a political offense such as rebellion.

assessor A local official who sets a value on property for tax purposes.

bankruptcy The legal process by which a person or company that cannot pay its debts has a court decide how the person or company's financial matters should be run to pay off the money owed or how the remaining property should be distributed among those to whom money is owed. Once the process is complete, the person or company is legally free of past debts.

benefit of clergy The centuries-old privilege that a member of the clergy used to have of being exempt from the penalty of execution. In medieval times, their cases could then be moved from a government court to a church court. Originally, this privilege had applied only to the clergy, then to anyone holding any kind of minor church job. Finally, the privilege was extended to those who could prove they could read. The purpose of benefit of clergy became that of lessening the extreme harshness of criminal laws. This privilege was ended by law in the United States in 1790.

billet An official order directing that a member of a military force be provided with food and lodging.

commons A piece of land set aside for common public use, especially for pasture.

constable A public officer usually of a town, whose job is similar to that of a sheriff, although the constable's powers are less. A constable is reponsible for keeping the peace and for minor judicial duties.

countersuit A legal action taken in a court for the recovery of a right or a claim, carried out in response to another's lawsuit.

countinghouse An office once used for keeping money account records and for transacting business.

dame school A school in which the basics of reading and writing are taught by a woman in her own home.

deacon A church officer or a member of a church's clergy or someone elected by church members to serve in worship, in care of members of the congregation, and on administrative committees.

debtors' prison A jail into which people who did not pay their debts were put. They stayed until their family or friends came up with the money to pay the debt.

divine right of kings The right of a monarch to rule as set forth in the theory that a king or queen receives the right to rule directly from God and not from the people.

duty A tax on imported or exported goods.

effigy An image or dummy of a hated person; the effigy was often hanged or burned in order to protest the hated person's activities.

grammar school A school emphasizing the learning of Latin and Greek in preparation for college.

green A commons or park in the center of a village or town.

indentured servant A person who signed and was bound by a contract to serve another for a specified period, especially in return for payment of travel expenses to the colony or place of work and for food and lodging.

inflation A general increase in the average prices of goods and services.

manslaughter The unlawful but unintentional killing of another person, done without malice.

militia Temporary citizen-soldiers called for service in emergencies, in contrast to regular troops.

monopoly Nearly total ownership or control of something because of legal privileges, power over supply, or group action.

naval stores Products such as turpentine and pitch obtained from trees, especially pines, which were used in the construction and maintenance of wooden sailing vessels.

nonimportation agreement An agreement not to import, that is, bring into the country, goods from specific other countries.

open letter A published letter of protest or appeal usually addressed to a specific person but really intended for the general public.

privateer An armed private ship hired by a government to attack the merchant ships and warships of an enemy.

proprietor A person who was given ownership of a colony and given the rights to establish a government and distribute land.

quartering Providing living quarters—lodging—to members of a military force.

radicals People supporting political views, practices, and policies of extreme change.

resolves Formal, legal, and official resolutions or statements.

scavenger A person hired to remove dirt and trash from the streets.

standing army A permanent army of paid soldiers.

tariff A duty or tax placed on imported or exported goods.

BIBLIOGRAPHY

and Recommended Readings

Adams, Samuel. *The Writings of Samuel Adams.* Ed. Harry Alonzo Cushing. 4 vol. 1907. New York: Octagon Reprint 1968.

*Alderman, Clifford Lindsay. *Samuel Adams, Son of Liberty.* New York: Holt Rinehart Winston, 1961.

Beach, Steward. *Samuel Adams, The Fateful Years 1764-1776.* New York: Dodd, Mead, 1965.

Butterfield, L. H. Ed. *The Adams Papers.* 4 vol. Cambridge: Belknap, 1961.

*Chidsey, Donald Barr. *The World of Samuel Adams.* New York: Nelson, 1974.

*Forbes, Esther. *Paul Revere and the World He Lived In.* Boston: Houghton, Mifflin, 1942.

Fowler, William M. Jr. *The Baron of Beacon Hill.* New York: Houghton, Mifflin, 1988.

Hosmer, James K. *Samuel Adams.* Boston: Houghton, Mifflin, 1899.

Miller, John C. *Sam Adams: Pioneer In Propaganda.* Stanford: Stanford University Press, 1936.

Russell, Frances. *Adams, An American Dynasty.* New York: American Heritage, 1976.

Wells, William V. *The Life and Public Services of Samuel Adams.* 3 vol. 1865-1888. Freeport, N.Y.: Books for Libraries Press. Reprint, 1969.

Willison, George F. *Patrick Henry and His World.* New York: Doubleday, 1969.

*Especially recommended for younger readers.

Boston, Massachusetts

- Samuel Adams's grave in Old Granary Burying Ground, Tremont Street.

- Samuel Adams's portrait by Copley at the Museum of Fine Arts, Huntington Avenue.

- Boston Common bounded by Boyleston, Charles, Beacon, Park, and Tremont Streets.

- Boston Latin School on School Street.

- Boston Massacre Site at Congress and State Streets.

- Boston Tea Party Ship Replica and Museum at Congress Street Bridge.

- Faneuil Hall and Museum on Congress Street.

- New State House on Beacon and Park Streets.

- Old North Church on Salem Street.

- Old South Meeting House on Washington Street.

- Old State House and Museum on State and Washington Streets.

- Paul Revere's House on North Square.

Charlestown, Massachusetts • Bunker Hill Monument on Breed's Hill.

Concord, Massachusetts • Minute Man National Historical Park in Concord, Lexington, and Lincoln.

Lexington, Massachusetts • Lexington Battle Green with tours of Buckman Tavern, Hancock-Clarke House, and Monroe Tavern. The Lexington Chamber of Commerce contains a diorama of the battle.

INDEX

124

Karin Clafford Farley is a lifelong resident of the Chicago area. She earned her bachelor's and master's degrees at the University of Illinois. Currently, she is a member of the faculty at the College of DuPage. Among previous books by the author are *Thomas Paine: Revolutionary Author* in the American Troublemakers series; *Canal Boy,* a story about President James A. Garfield—20th President of the United States; *Harry S. Truman, The Man from Independence*; and *Robert H. Goddard*—a biography of the father of rocketry.

James P. Shenton is Professor of History at Columbia University. He has taught American History since 1951. Among his publications are *Robert John Walker, a Politician from Jackson to Lincoln*; *An Historian's History of the United States*; and *The Melting Pot*. Professor Shenton is a consultant to the National Endowment for the Humanities and has received the Mark Van Doren and Society of Columbia Graduates' Great Teachers Awards. He also serves as a consultant for CBS, NBC, and ABC educational programs.